T0114474

The Psychology of Music

How does music affect our moods? What is the best way to develop musical skills? How does the definition of music vary between cultures?

The Psychology of Music explores the important impact music has on our everyday lives, and its influence on society, groups and individual people. It demonstrates how music can benefit our intellectual functioning, and health and well-being, and examines musical ability as both a gift and something that can be developed through learning and practice.

Music can enhance our understanding of humanity and modern life and The Psychology of Music shows us the significance of music, and the power it can have over our behaviour.

Susan Hallam is Emerita Professor of Education and Music Psychology at the UCL Institute of Education. She was awarded an MBE in the 2015 New Year's Honours list and pursued careers as both a professional musician and a music educator before becoming an academic.

THE PSYCHOLOGY OF EVERYTHING

The Psychology of Everything is a series of books which debunk the myths and pseudo-science surrounding some of life's biggest questions.

The series explores the hidden psychological factors that drive us, from our sub-conscious desires and aversions, to the innate social instincts handed to us across the generations. Accessible, informative, and always intriguing, each book is written by an expert in the field, examining how research-based knowledge compares with popular wisdom, and illustrating the potential of psychology to enrich our understanding of humanity and modern life.

Applying a psychological lens to an array of topics and contemporary concerns – from sex to addiction to conspiracy theories – *The Psychology of Everything* will make you look at everything in a new way.

Titles in the series:

For further information about this series please visit:
www.thepsychologyofeverything.co.uk

The Psychology of Music

Susan Hallam

Routledge
Taylor & Francis Group

LONDON AND NEW YORK

First published 2019
by Routledge
2 Park Square, Milton Park, Abingdon, Oxon OX14 4RN

and by Routledge
605 Third Avenue, New York, NY 10017

Routledge is an imprint of the Taylor & Francis Group, an informa business

British Library Cataloguing-in-Publication Data
A catalogue record for this book is available from the British Library

Library of Congress Cataloging-in-Publication Data
A catalog record for this book has been requested

ISBN 13: 978-1-138-09847-3 (hbk)
ISBN 13: 978-1-138-09854-1 (pbk)
ISBN 13: 978-1-315-10436-2 (ebk)

Typeset in Joanna
by Apex CoVantage, LLC

Contents

1

Music, its significance and functions

What is music? What we define as music is culturally and individu-ally determined. Of course, sound exists as an objective reality but for that sound to be considered as music we need to recognise it as such. What is acknowledged as 'music' varies between cultures, sub-cultures and individuals. The music of one culture or sub-culture may not be recognised as music by members of others. A relatively culturally neutral definition of music is 'the art or science of arranging sounds in notes and rhythms to give a desired pattern or effect'.[1] In Western cultures, historically greater account was taken of the aes-thetic qualities of music. One definition described it as 'the art of combining sounds of voice(s) or instrument(s) to achieve beauty of form and expression of emotion'.[2] Of course, defining music in these terms depends on personal judgements of what constitutes beauty of form and expression of emotion. This varies. Indeed, what constitutes 'music' for some would not be described by others as either beautiful or expressive of emotion. Within this frame of reference, you may wish to consider which genres or styles you would describe as music.

In non-Western cultures, music can have very different mean-ings. In some, the concept of music is integrated with dance, for instance, the Igbo of Nigeria have no specific term for music; the term nkwa denotes 'singing, playing instruments and dancing'.[3] In some cultures, music making is a collective activity where every-body actively participates. This contrasts with Western classical music where there are clearly defined roles for performers and audiences, although this is less the case for non-classical music where audiences may participate in singing and moving to the music. Overall, music cannot be understood in isolation from the context in which it occurs. Culture shapes music, while music, in turn, influences human behaviour. From this perspective we might think of music as 'sound that is organised into socially accepted patterns'.[4] However, in modern, multi-cultural societies, where the music that is socially accepted varies between sub-groups and may also differ between individuals within them, a contemporary definition may be that music is sound which is organised into patterns which are socially or individually accepted.

The universality of music

However we choose to define music, it is universal and found in all cultures. It is the very essence of humanity. It rewards, clarifies and enhances shared feelings and experiences. Throughout the ages it has played a significant role in the lives of people all over the world.[5] Despite this, specific universal characteristics of music and music making have proved difficult to identify, although music is valued universally for its impact on the emotions. Singing is universal, and most cultures use instruments. Other possible universals are the presence of some kind of pulse; the division of musical sequences into smaller groups of phrases; the equivalence of pitches which are separated by an octave (a series of eight notes occupying the interval between and including two notes, one having twice or half the frequency of vibration of the other); the presence of the perfect fifth (the interval from the first to the last of five consecutive notes in a diatonic scale); and the organisation of pitch into some kind of typically asymmetric tonal system (in Western music the diatonic scale, which includes five whole steps and two half steps in each octave). Overall, however, there are no elements which are consistently shared.[6]

Currently, it is not possible to say with any confidence whether music is the product of culturally learned norms or of universally shared neural and cognitive processes. It is most likely that it is based on an interaction between the two.

An alternative approach to considering the universal characteristics of music is to explore the extent to which music expresses similar emotions. Music of different cultures may communicate common emotions, but through different tonal and rhythmic structures. Certainly, music has the power to express and evoke a wide range of emotions. Songs across the world focus on important, shared human experiences, for instance, friendship, joy, comfort, knowledge, religion and love. These themes, along with songs for children, including lullabies and play songs, are found in all cultures and seem to be universal.[7]

Music as unique to human beings

Alongside the debate about what might constitute universality in music is the question of whether music is unique to humans. Are the sounds that animals make music? Do animals respond to and make music? With regard to the first of these questions, whether we perceive the sounds that animals make, for instance, bird song as music, is very much dependent on our personal tastes. The answer to the second question is more complex. There is some evidence that animals respond to music. For instance, there is much anecdotal evidence that cows produce more milk when music is playing in the background. This may be because the music reduces stress which can inhibit the release of oxytocin, a hormone which is key to the milk-releasing process. There is also evidence that birds which can mimic human sounds can move in time to music at different tempi.[8] Bio-musicologists argue that animal sounds comprise the same musical language as that used by humans. For instance, birds have developed similar pitch and rhythm patterns to humans, while whales use many of the musical concepts found in human music, including similar rhythms, phrase lengths and song structure.[9] However, our nearest primate relatives demonstrate few capabilities that could be inter-preted as musical. They do not have the capacity to produce complex vocal signals and there is no evidence that they can move in time to a beat.[5] Generally, even among primates, vocal signals tend to be closely linked to specific communication circumstances.[10] Currently, the jury is still out as to whether animals share similar capacities for making music as humans.

The evolutionary significance of music

A further debate centres on whether music has evolutionary sig-nificance. Answers to this question are inevitably speculative. One argument suggests that music exemplifies many of the classic criteria for a complex human evolutionary adaptation. No culture has ever been without music (universality); musical development in children tends to follow broadly the same pattern; musicality is widespread (all adults can appreciate music and remember tunes); there is specialist memory for music; specialised cortical mechanisms in the brain are involved; there are parallels in the signals of other species, e.g. birds, gibbons and whales; and music can evoke strong emotions which implies adaptive behaviours relating to listening and making music.[11]

If music does have an evolutionary origin, what might it be? The main theoretical positions suggest that music may have evolved in relation to the following:

- mate selection, as an element of courtship behaviour;
- social cohesion, creating or maintaining social cohesion through the promotion of group solidarity and altruism;
- group effort, contributing to the co-ordination of group work;
- perceptual development, contributing towards the more general development of sound perception;
- motor skill development, through singing with movement and other music making providing opportunities for refining motor skills;

- conflict reduction, reducing interpersonal conflict within groups through shared activities which are unlikely to provoke argument or dispute;
- safe time passing, providing a way of passing time which avoids engagement with possible dangerous situations; and
- trans-generational communication, providing a useful memory device for passing on information from generation to generation.[12]

Several theories focus on music's importance in relation to social cohesion, promoting co-operative behaviour and synchronising the emotions of many individuals who can then collectively take action to protect and defend themselves.[13] The downside of this is that it also has the potential for developing feelings of hostility towards outgroups. The multi-faceted nature of music making also supports the development of a wide range of important life skills simultaneously, including the development of language; listening, monitoring and evaluation skills; concentration; communication; perception of mood and emotion; and physical skills. Overall, making music involves many different parts of the brain and may have played a unique role in facilitating the acquisition and maintenance of the skill of being a member of a culture, helping us to interact with others socially and providing us with the intellectual skills which distinguish us from other species.[14] This is supported by the evidence of the existence of music many thousands of years ago. The earliest musical instrument found was a 53,000–year–old bone flute, rather like a modern recorder, made from an animal leg bone. This was a sophisticated instrument and showed that time and effort had gone into its creation, suggesting that music was important within that culture.[9]

Not all authors agree that music has evolutionary purpose. Some suggest that music, along with the other arts, has no evolutionary significance and no practical function. Music has been condemned as an evolutionary parasite[15] and as auditory cheesecake,[16] an evolutionary by-product of the emergence of other capacities that have direct adaptive value. From this perspective music exists simply because of the pleasure that it affords. Whatever the origins of music, there is no doubt that engagement with it is rewarding for human beings as a species. If this were not the case, individuals would not spend so much time engaged in musical activity.

The functions of music in society today

Music has many different functions in the modern world. These operate at several levels, that of the individual, the social group and society in general, and vary within and between cultures.

The functions of music at the individual level

At the individual level music is a vehicle for emotional expression. We can express ideas and emotions through music which we might find difficult to convey in ordinary verbal interchanges. Love songs, those expressing anguish at broken relationships or grief following bereavement are all examples of the way that music helps us to express complex emotions. Music changes our arousal levels. We use music to relax and to motivate us when we take exercise. Music is effective in changing our moods and emotions. We take advantage of its easy availability[17] and use it to manipulate how we feel (see Chapter 4). We may play lively music to prepare us for going to a party, sad music to help us work through difficult emotions, or calming music when we are feeling stressed. Music enables us to express our identity. The kind of music that we listen to indicates something about our lifestyle and beliefs. This is particularly evident in the teenage years where music, dress, our friends and the kind of activities we engage with enable us to tell the world who we are. It is used on online dating sites as one element of creating a good match. Music entertains us and provides us with aesthetic enjoyment through concert attendance, listening to recordings or making music. Actively making music provides us with challenge, stimulates us intellectually, physically and emotionally and we experience reward when we achieve or perform successfully. In addition, musical activities may improve a range of transferable skills including concentration, self-discipline, physical co-ordination and literacy skills[18] (see Chapter 8).

The functions of music at the group level

Music fulfils important functions for groups. It provides an alternative means of communication as meanings, understandings and experiences are shared. For instance, historically, music was used in battle to co-ordinate movement, create a shared purpose and help overcome fear. Music binds social groups together and supports developing identities. Football fans have songs dedicated to their teams as do some organisations, for instance, schools, youth groups. Adolescents are in part defined by their music. It creates a social badge reflecting their chosen youth culture, in some cases one that is perceived negatively by some, for instance, heavy metal and rap/hip hop. Historically, music has been used in work contexts, for instance, the BBC programme 'Music while you Work' consisted of lively music designed to motivate workers on production lines to maintain high levels of productivity, while sometimes it helps individuals literally work in time together, for instance, in marching or rowing. With the increase in office-based work, now it is more likely that individuals will promote their concentration by listening to music of their choice on head phones rather than there being a shared musical environment. Emotional expression is important at the group level, for instance, in protest songs where music has contributed to raising issues about nuclear armament, the Vietnam war or environmental destruction. Music plays a role in most religious worship through the singing of hymns and chanting and can contribute to meditation. It helps us to experience and express spiritual concerns in a way that words cannot. Music is frequently present when we celebrate, for instance, at weddings or birthdays. It is a powerful way of expressing happiness and thanksgiving, particularly when it is accompanied by dancing. Equally it is present at funerals, when it allows us to express grief. When communities undergo periods of change, music can provide continuity, for instance for refugees and immigrants.

The functions of music in society

In society as a whole, music provides a means of symbolic representation for other things, ideas and behaviours. It can, for instance, represent the state, national or regional identity (with national or regional anthems); patriotism; bravery; heroism; rebellion (through songs); and religion (hymns, chants). Conformity to social norms can be encouraged through ballads which can provide warnings to others. Music supports all major ceremonial occasions, e.g. state weddings, military functions, funerals, national sporting events. Who could forget Luciano Pavarotti performing 'Nessun Dorma' at the 1990 FIFA World Cup final or Elton John singing 'Candle in the wind' at the funeral of Princess Diana? As we respond to the music of our culture in similar ways, it contributes towards continuity and stability and the integration and cohesion of society.

The power of music is reflected in the way that the state may attempt to exert control over it. In Nazi Germany music was carefully selected for use at mass rallies to generate appropriate patriotic emotions. During the Cultural Revolution in China, Western music was denounced as decadent and forbidden. In modern-day Russia, members of the punk band Pussy Riot were sentenced to two years in prison after being arrested on hooliganism charges for performing in Moscow's Cathedral of Christ the Saviour in 2012. In the same year Lady Gaga was forced to cancel a sold-out performance in Indonesia after Islamic conservatives protested that her mode of dress and dance would corrupt the country's youth.

Music not only serves a range of functions in societies, but its nature reflects the values, attitudes and characteristics of that society. For instance, the Western classical tradition reflected a drive to rationalise and understand the environment. The development of systems of musical notation extended what could be passed on to future generations, at a time when oral cultures restricted what could be remembered. Recent recording techniques now mean that music can be passed on without notation. This in turn has led to a greater emphasis on professional musicians being able to play by ear. Technological advances have impacted on the availability of music in our everyday lives, the extent to which we can access music from other cultures, how musical skills are developed and the ways in which music can be performed enabling performances from individuals or groups in separate locations to be co-ordinated.

Psychology of music

The psychology of music, or music psychology as it is sometimes known, has a long history beginning with the ancient Greeks. Pythagoras (580–500 BCE), perhaps better known for his theorem relating to triangles, conducted a series of experiments with a monochord (a one stringed instrument) that laid the ground work for music theory and the inclusion of music in the early Greek education system as a mathematical science along with arithmetic, geometry and astronomy. Modern music psychology emerged in the 19th century and had a particular emphasis on understanding the properties of sound and the measurement and nature of musical ability (see Chapter 6). From the 1960s onwards, the field grew to include research on music perception (particularly of pitch, rhythm, harmony and melody) and how we respond to it (see Chapter 2); musical development including our musical preferences (see Chapter 3) and the learning and performance of music (see Chapters 6 and 7). More recently there has been an emphasis on the impact of music on our emotions, and how we interact with music in our everyday lives (see Chapters 2 and 4) and the wider benefits of music to our health and well-being (see Chapter 5) and intellectual functioning (see Chapter 8).

Conclusions

What constitutes music is culturally and individually defined. While music is found in all cultures, it varies between them. For many years it was believed to be unique to human beings, although recent research has begun to question this. A wide range of evolutionary roles have been proposed for music, although it may simply be for our pleasure. Music has a range of functions in society, at the group level and for individuals. At the societal level it contributes to the continuity of cultural social norms, institutions and religion, while for groups within society it is important for defining group membership and maintaining cohesiveness. At the individual level, it has an impact on emotions, activity levels, well-being, communication and identity. Music psychology has a particular focus on the role of music for the individual and for groups within society including how we process sound, the impact on our emotions, daily lives and cognitive skills and how we develop general and specialist musical skills.

2

The processing of music

The ability to process sound is crucial for our survival. We process sounds even when we are asleep. It is therefore not surprising that we have robust sound processing systems. It is so important that the structures in the brain for processing sound are operational before we are born (see Chapter 3). The neural systems for processing music are widely distributed throughout the brain but there are also locally specialised regions. Some neural networks are specific to music while others are shared with other networks including those for language.

Music listening skills do not need to be taught. When we listen to music we process an enormous amount of information rapidly and often without conscious awareness. The ease with which we do this depends on our prior musical experiences and the culturally determined tonal scheme to which we have become accustomed. This knowledge is implicit (not always available to conscious thought) and is applied automatically whenever we listen to music. This ability to listen to and process music is acquired automatically through exposure to music in much the same way that language, for instance English, Spanish, Mandarin, is acquired through exposure. In this way we acquire knowledge of musical regularities and structure.

When we are listening, the processing of music seems effortless. However, we are engaged in analysing, segmenting and encoding a complex stream of sound. We have to perceive and understand individual sounds and phrases as they connect to create longer musical events and remember important themes and patterns. This goes on without our conscious awareness. The process is automated. Musical training is not necessary for this to occur, although musical experience leads to greater sophistication in our implicit musical knowledge. Because these skills are acquired so easily, there has been a tendency to underestimate the musical capabilities of people who have not had formal training.

There are only minor differences in musical processing between those with formal training and those who are untrained. Non-musicians find it more difficult to recognise the intervals between notes and differentiate between the notes in a complex chord. They are also slower in identifying musical themes. Despite this, to some extent, they possess absolute pitch (see Chapter 6). They remember tempos at the same speed and melodies at the same pitch as recordings that they have listened to frequently.[1] Overall, the human brain has a predisposition for processing music without training which is enhanced by living in a rich musical environment.[2] The type of musical environment to which we are exposed in childhood varies enormously (see Chapter 3), and as we grow older we make choices about the extent to which we want to engage with music. Some choose to actively make music, playing or singing while others prefer to spend time listening. The nature of these activities has an impact on the processing and understanding of music.

Have you had musical training of any kind? If so, do you think it changed the way that you listen to music? If so what did it change?

Music processing and the brain

The way that we process music requires neural activity across many areas of the brain including auditory association areas in the temporal lobes, auditory working memory areas in the frontal lobes, and emotional centres in the limbic system. Research with those who have brain damage has shown that musical functions can be left unchanged or impaired depending on the nature of the damage. Loss of musical function, amusia, is often accompanied by aphasia (loss of language functions) but each can occur in the absence of the other. A range of musical functions can be disrupted by brain damage, for instance, playing an instrument, producing and matching sounds, identifying or singing well-known melodies, reading musical notation, perceiving rhythms, discriminating differences in pitch loudness, duration, timbre and rhythm and copying notation. This diversity illustrates the extent to which music-related behaviours are distributed across both cerebral hemispheres.[3]

One important question is whether there are cultural differences in the ways that people process music where there are different tonal and rhythmic systems. The evidence to date suggests that the brain is sensitive to music of specific genres and familiar rather than unfamiliar instruments but that the basic processes involved are the same.[4]

The processing of music

When we listen to music we have to group incoming sounds into a series of events and sequences. In Western tonal music, a range of cues assist in this process, differences in pitch, similarity of timbre (quality of sound), closeness in time and similarity in the extent of vibration.[5] This level of analysis has been conceptualised as 'auditory scene analysis'. This is how the human auditory system organises sound into meaningful units. The important principles underpinning this process are the grouping of similar or proximate objects together across time, melody, frequency and harmony.

We develop automaticity in processing music through the brain's ability to internalise statistical regularities as it is exposed to different sounds. When a particular sound occurs frequently in the environment the neural networks which support its perception become stronger. This supports the development of schemata. These are learned patterns which form mental representations of basic music elements. These change as we gain musical experience and enable us to make sense of music. As we learn more we become able to focus attention on different schema and to separate out different strands of the music. We tend to do this when the sounds are very different, for instance, large variations in pitch, rhythm, pulse or timbre (frequently the sounds made by different instruments). As we listen we can choose which stream to attend to. For instance, in Tchaikovsky's 1812 overture one could choose to focus on the Marseillaise representing the French under Napoleon or the theme that represents the Russian forces. This is an example of counterpoint, where two sound streams are harmonically inter-related, but differ in rhythm and melody. Counterpoint is common in the music of Bach (see, for instance, the Prelude and Fugue No. 13 in F-Sharp Major, BWV 858).

The processing of rhythm, pulse and metre

The processing of time in music is generally conceptualised in terms of rhythm, pulse and metre. Rhythm is the way that patterns of time intervals are sequenced. It is the central organising structure of music. Much music also has a sense of pulse or beat, which changes depending on the tempo (speed) of the music. Beats divide the music into equal or unequal units. Metre refers to the way in which the stresses of the beats are organised. For instance, in a waltz, the stress is on the first of every three beats, while in a march and most popular music every other beat is emphasised. Not all cultures share conceptualisations of regular beats and metre, for instance, the 'tala' in North Indian music has metre but does not necessarily have a regularly recurring pattern. These differences mean that listeners from diverse cultures may perceive temporal structures in different ways.

The processing of rhythm, pulse and metre require different computational processes. When we process rhythm, we have to analyse different time intervals which vary in length. Processing tempo requires us to represent the frequency rates of the pulse. This depends on a relatively simple analysis and activates comparatively old neural systems in the brain. Processing metre requires us to represent repeating cycles of strong and weak beats. This engages older systems in the brain (e.g. basal ganglia) and higher cognitive systems (e.g.

pre-frontal systems involved in executive function). As we hear music, activations representing each of these occur within the same time frame. Try listening to piece of music and see which you are most easily able to identify. Is one more dominant than the other?

Moving in synchrony to rhythm occurs across cultures and without training. We spontaneously co-ordinate our movements with complex musical rhythms, for instance, tapping our feet. This is known as entrainment. This is a highly complex activity, which involves auditory, visual, proprioceptive (the sense of how your limbs are oriented in space) and vestibular (balance, orientation in space) perception. Several models attempt to explain how we process pulse and metre, some of which are based on entrainment. For instance, neural resonance theory suggests that perception of pulse and metre correspond to rhythms in the brain.[6] Other models focus on the rules that underpin processing.

Tonality, pitch, melody and harmony

Our processing of music depends, to a great extent, on tonal structure and melodic contour. In Western genres tonality is a common central organising factor. Pitch is broken into discrete steps to form scales the most common being diatonic and chromatic scales. Other cultures have different scales, for instance, the Indian raga, the Balinese slendro and pelog of gamelan music and the Persian dastgah. Most scales use intervals of nonequal size and are formed from a set of twelve pitches with several subsets of seven pitches which each define a musical key. In Western tonal music keys are defined in terms of a specific tone, the tonic. This is the most important reference point for processing most Western music. It anchors all other tones.

Melody is perceived through auditory grouping where successive notes are put together to form a perception of contour.[7] Notes are more likely to be grouped into the same stream when they are close together in pitch or time. Vertical grouping produces harmony where tones are grouped to form chords. In much music, some chords are more important than others, typically, the tonic and those based on the fourth or fifth of the scale. Much popular music is based on these three chords, examples include 'Home on the Range' and Bob Dylan's 'Blowing in the Wind'.

There are two main models which explain tonal hierarchy. Tonal Pitch Space theory[8] suggests that listeners hear pitches and chords as relatively close or distant from a given tonic in an orderly way. The other, based on a neural network model,[9] suggests that a tri-level system links tones, chords and keys in a hierarchical order. There may be some basic properties of our auditory and processing systems which determine why some combinations of notes sound more harmonious than others, although it may be that we learn these as we acquire the tonal system of our culture and it is familiarity with them which makes them preferable to dissonant patterns. It has been suggested, for instance, that if we were brought up listening to atonal music, we would perceive it as harmonious. Try listening to Schoenberg's song cycle *Pierrot Lunaire* (1912) or Alban Berg's opera *Wozzeck* (1925) and see what you think.

The perception of timbre

Timbre is the character or quality of a musical sound or voice. The processing of timbre is one of the ways that we can track different sound sources independently. Timbre may be produced by a single sound source or a number operating together, for instance, different combinations of instruments. It can contribute to expressiveness in music enhancing tension and relaxation. Non-musicians are more sensitive to changes in timbre than pitch.[10]

The processing of large musical forms

When we listen to music, particularly long pieces, we need to be able to identify which parts are the most important. Some parts are structurally important, while others are merely ornamental.[11] The generative theory of tonal music[12] sets out how we do this, through identifying the rules of musical grammar. Four types of hierarchical structure have been proposed:

- grouping structures (the way we segment music into motifs, phrases and sections);
- metrical structure (strong and weak beats);
- time span reduction (the link between pitch and rhythm, the structural importance of rhythmic events);
- prolongation reduction (a hierarchy of tension-release patterns).

An alternative theory focuses on cue abstraction.[13] This suggests that as we listen we segment music into different lengths based on differences and similarities and through this create memory units that integrate the features of the musical style.

Memory for music

Remembering lengthy sequences of music is a complex process. We generally remember music without thinking about how we do it (see also Chapter 7). The schemata that we develop in relation to the tonality, rhythm, pulse and metre of our culture form the basis for our musical memories. The memories that we have for specific music are integrated into this musical framework. We remember music that we have heard frequently. The more often we listen to a piece of music the stronger the neural networks that support its perception. We seem to remember familiar tunes in a relatively abstract way as we still recognise them when they are played at different pitches, tempo or by different instruments.[1] As we repeatedly listen to a piece of music we gain a greater understanding of its structure and the relationship of themes within it. We also remember factual information about music but in different parts of the brain from the memories for the music itself.

Do you sometimes find that a piece of music that you have listened to keeps going round in your head even when you are no longer listening to it? This phenomenon is known as having an ear worm. They typically occur in relation to familiar and recently listened to pieces of music although they can be triggered by other experiences, for instance, a word or a few notes from the song or feeling an emotion associated with it.[14] Almost everyone experiences earworms, although they tend to last for longer in women who also find them more irritating than men.[15]

Responses to music

When you listen to music how do you react to it? Do your moods and behaviour change? Do you find yourself trying to work out the structure of the music, or what instruments are involved? Human beings respond to music in a variety of different ways: physiologically, through movement, through changes in behaviour, aesthetically, intellectually and through changes in mood, arousal levels and emotions. The next sections explore these issues. As you are reading you may wish to reflect on the different ways that you respond to music.

Physiological responses to music

The effects of music on a range of physiological responses including heart rate, respiration, blood pressure, muscular tension, movement, posture and stomach contractions have all been investigated. No clear patterns relating music to physiological measures have been found. We might expect that fast, loud, exciting music would lead to an increase in physiological measures, but this is not always the case. Similarly, calming music does not always lead to a reduction in physiological response, although frequently it does. This may be because our responses are affected by other factors, for instance, our liking for particular pieces of music, the connections they have with events in our lives, how often we listen to music, whether we have musical training and our personality. Music also has a positive impact on the neurochemical systems involved in the reward and pleasure systems in the brain.[1]

Movement

Many musical experiences involve movement. The relationship between movement and music begins in infancy with the co-ordinated movements of mothers and other adults with babies. Adults sing lullabies while rocking infants and bounce them while singing play songs. Music and movement have always played a central role in bringing up children, social bonding and in everyday life. Music generates movement through dance and a range of activities related to courtship, celebration and worship. The movement that accompanies music is an integral part of the musical experience and cannot be separated from it.

The effects on behaviour

Music affects our behaviour. It can act as a stimulus to movement, or relaxation. Young children become more active when lively music is playing. We use music to relax, and to support a range of fitness activities, although the impact here is mainly related to motivation rather than having a specific impact on the activity itself. An extreme example of the effect of music on behaviour is the part it plays in creating trance-like states. The impact of music on behaviour will be discussed further in Chapter 4.

Aesthetic responses to music

Aesthetic responses are subjective, personal responses to beauty or ugliness. They depend on the taste and judgement of each listener. They differ from emotional responses in that they require us to evaluate the music. While there is a tendency to conceptualise aesthetic responses as only being relevant to high art, some have argued that aesthetic experience can be applied to reactions to any form of art. So the reaction of a popular music fan to the latest release of their favourite artist is no different to the response of a highly trained musician to a new musical composition. Exploration of the neural systems which underpin aesthetic experience[16] has shown at least three different kinds of identifiable brain activity are involved: the enhancement of low-level sensory processing; high-level, top-down processing and the activation of cortical areas involved in evaluative judgements; and engagement of the reward circuits in the brain. Aesthetic judgements may have evolutionary significance as the cortical regions involved in evaluations of art overlap with those required for judgements made about food and mate selection.[17] What kinds of music would you describe as beautiful? Is there some music that you really enjoy listening to that you would not describe as beautiful? What is it about that music that draws you to listen to it?

Intellectual stimulation

Music can be a source of intellectual stimulation. Listening to music, identifying its structures and forms, analysing it, learning about its history and forms across different cultures, learning to play an instrument or sing, composing, improvising and performing all offer intellectual stimulation and challenge. These are relevant across the lifespan and are not restricted to experiences in formal education or being actively engaged in making music. For instance, collectors of recordings of music are partially motivated by a desire to expand their knowledge and understanding of music.[18]

Moods and arousal levels

We frequently use music to explore and regulate our moods. In fact, the most common activity for regulating our moods is listening to music.[18] Generally, slow, quiet music reduces anxiety and helps us to relax, while stimulating music tends to increase our arousal levels, although it has proved difficult to specify with any degree of accuracy which musical structures evoke which moods and emotions. Exploration of gender, age or social class differences has revealed no clear patterns, although some studies have shown that there are effects of formal training. Overall, quite different types of music can change mood in the same direction. This may be because the individual characteristics of the listener and their prior experiences with music are important mediators. For instance, favourite music of whatever type can lower feelings of tension while physiological responses tend to be greater during exciting music regardless of whether listeners like it or not.

Music does not always have a positive impact. For instance, adolescents may use music as a distraction, to avoid thinking about problems leading to a negative impact on their psychological adjustment. Listening to music that explores negative themes, for instance distress, suicide, or death, can increase depressive symptoms and suicidal thoughts.[18]

Emotional responses to music

As we saw in Chapter 1, most people can recognise the emotions which a particular piece of music from their own culture is trying to portray and sometimes they can do this in relation to music from other cultures. Making links between particular musical events and the perception of emotion has proved difficult. Any musical structure may represent a number of different emotional expressions. Perceived expression is never determined by a single musical event but is a function of many interacting together. Overall, the way in which music represents emotion may never be captured in a strict scientific sense.[19]

While we may be able to identify the emotion that music is trying to portray, this does not mean that we experience that emotion. There is wide variability in our emotional responses to music. These depend on complex socio-cultural, historical, educational and contextual variables. While experiences with music may influence our moods, they may not have an impact on our emotions.[20]

Some individuals have very strong responses to music including, chills, crying, lump in the throat, shivering, prickly feeling on the back of the neck, tingling along the spine, goose bumps. The exact relationship between such experiences and emotions is unclear.[21] Some listeners report 'peak' emotional experiences. The most common include exhilaration, joy and ecstasy. Less common are quasi-physical, perceptual, cognitive, existential, transcendental and religious experiences.[19] Have you had any peak experiences with music? What were you listening to, playing or singing at the time? What elements of the music do you think brought about this experience?

Overall, there are three main explanations for our emotional responses to music. The first suggests that there are pre-wired connections between musical stimuli and emotional responses. In the same way that we might respond to a loud noise we respond immediately to the sound of music without conscious thought. As the music changes in tempo, dynamics, pitch and timbre, the changes are monitored and our autonomic nervous system responds. Exploration of strong positive emotional responses to music has demonstrated that the brain areas implicated are those which are activated in response to highly rewarding stimuli. Activity in relation to these reward processes is known to involve dopamine and opioid systems as well as other neurotransmitters. The amygdala, implicated in fear and negative emotions, also shows a decrease in activity as emotional responses become more intense. The powerful impact of music may be because it evokes some emotions while simultaneously inhibiting incompatible ones.[22]

The second explanation for our emotional responses is that there may be links with a specific emotional event in our lives, for instance, music playing when we first met a partner. The meanings which we attach to music can be absolute (internal to the music itself) or referential (referring to non-musical phenomenon).[23] Referential meanings relate to life events to which particular pieces of music are attached. For instance, music playing at the funeral of someone close to us may evoke tears when that music is heard again.

Thirdly, emotions may be aroused when musical expectations are disconfirmed or delayed.[23] Music sets up expectations and tensions. Depending on how these are realised or resolved they can create different emotional responses. Music generates expectations based on our knowledge of the tonality of our culture and common features of particular genres.[23] Variations in how these expectations are met or violated play a significant role in determining emotional responses to music. As a species we have evolved a brain which rewards accurate prediction of future events. Music seems to use this to generate emotional responses.[24] Brain mechanisms encode the recent past, predict the future and adjust encoding when predictions are inaccurate. These mechanisms, although largely cortically based, interact with the reward system leading to emotional responses. A challenge for expectancy theories is how we have emotional responses to music which we know well, i.e. we know what to expect. The explanation for this is that our reactions to unexpected events occur automatically, without attention so even when we know the music we continue to have an emotional response.[24] In Western tonal music, expectations are shaped by structures involving rhythm, metre, tonality, harmony and melody. These provide composers with many means of disconfirming expectations.

Several models have been developed to explain our overall emotional reactions to music. The most comprehensive is the BRECVEMA framework.[20] It includes eight elements:

Brain stem reflex: a hard-wired attention response to simple acoustic features such as extreme or increasing loudness or speed.

Rhythmic entrainment: a gradual adjustment of an internal body rhythm (e.g., heart rate) toward an external rhythm in the music.

Evaluative conditioning: a regular pairing of a piece of music and other positive or negative stimuli leading to a conditioned association.

Contagion: an internal 'mimicry' of the perceived voice-like emotional expression of the music.

Visual imagery: inner images of an emotional character conjured up by the listener through a metaphorical mapping of the musical structure.

Episodic memory: a conscious recollection of a particular event from the listener's past, triggered by the music.

Musical expectancy: a reaction to the gradual unfolding of the musical structure and its expected or unexpected continuation.

Aesthetic judgement: a subjective evaluation of the aesthetic value of the music based on an individual set of weighted criteria.

Conclusion

The processing of sound was crucial to our evolutionary survival and perhaps because of this, the mechanisms for processing sound are highly developed and operate automatically. When we listen to music our brains are engaged in undertaking complex analyses which involve many different neural areas. We are unaware of this as the process is automated and develops as we are exposed to music in the environment. Musical training is not required. Our responses to music take many forms: physiological; through changes in behaviour, movement, arousal levels, moods and emotions; and aesthetically and intellectually. This may be why music is so powerful and why many spend so much time listening to it. The positive impact it can have on our moods and emotions may be particularly important for our well-being.

3

The lifelong development of general musical skills

The way that our musical skills develop in the early years of our childhood depends on the environment we are brought up in. Think back to your early childhood. What music did you hear in your home? Did you actively make music with those who were caring for you? What impact did this have on you? Were there other environments which impacted on your musical development?

Several models have been developed to map the complex interactions that we have with our environment. Probably the most influential is that of Bronfenbrenner.[1] This model includes a micro system which sets out interactions between the individual and their immediate environment, a meso-system which refers to the individual's interactions within the wider environment and an exo-system where the individual does not interact with others directly but where someone close to the individual does so. The model also identifies a macro-system which encompasses the sub-culture in which the particular beliefs, values and ideologies of the other systems are embedded. These various systems influence the opportunities that we have to develop general musical skills. Helena Gaunt and I[2] used Bronfenbrenner's model to outline the possible influences on a teenager learning to play the guitar. These are set out in Figure 3.1. To what extent did these various systems impact on your musical development?

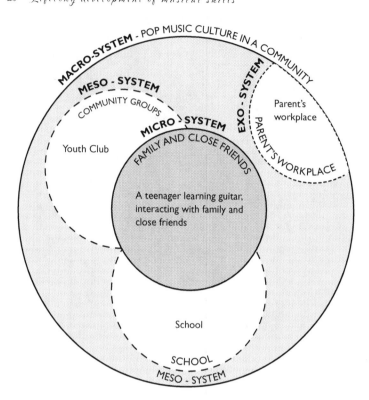

Figure 3.1 Possible macro-, meso- and exo-systems for a teenager learning to play the guitar

Of course, there are other factors which play a part in our musical development. These have been modelled by Hettema and Kenrick[3] who suggest six categories of interaction and their impact:

- static person-environment mesh where the individual is situated in an unchanging environment;
- choice of environments by persons where the individual selects new environments which meet his/her needs;
- choice of persons by environments which is typified by a variety of selection processes, for instance in education and the work place;

- transformation of environments by persons where individuals through their actions change environments, for instance, through leadership or disruption;
- transformation of persons by environments where individuals are socialised into new environments; and
- person-environment transactions or mutual transactions in which both persons and environments change over time.

Each of these categories represents different degrees of fit and influence between the individual and the environment. They form the basis for our individual development trajectories. These kinds of interactions are demonstrated in Figures 3.2 and 3.3, which show how these might operate within the broader ecological system in relation to a child who has an interest in playing popular music. Looking at each of these figures can you identify where you chose environments conducive to your musical development, or where environments rejected you?

As we shall see in Chapter 6, historically, it was generally believed that musical ability was inherited and that this determined what any of us could achieve. However, recent genetic research has acknowledged the important role that experience has in determining our behaviour and also in modifying the behaviour of genes.[4] Alongside this, research in neuroscience has demonstrated the extent of plasticity in the brain[5] and the extent to which the specific musical activities that we are engaged in have a very specific impact on the brain. For instance, there will be differences in the brains of violinists, percussionists and conductors because of the very different skills that they have acquired.[6]

The way that we each develop musically can be considered as a trajectory from a continuum of musical possibilities. As we proceed along our trajectory the interactions that we have with others changes. This in turn impacts on future trajectories. For instance, if as a parent you perceive that your child is interested in music you are likely to provide opportunities for him/her to engage in musical activities. If your child finds the musical activity interesting and

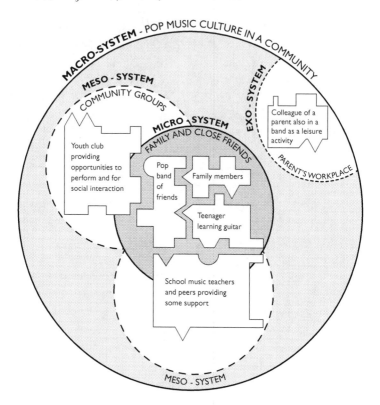

Figure 3.2 Systemic and bio-social developmental interactions for a teenager learning to play the guitar

rewarding this encourages greater interest and engagement which leads to you further supporting his/her musical development. This in turn leads to changes in the brain which facilitate further learning. As there is huge variability in the kinds of musical opportunities which are available, initially to young children and later throughout the lifespan, the potential for diversity in individual musical developmental trajectories is very great. Take a moment to think about your musical trajectory. Can you map out the various influences and opportunities which may have had a major impact on your musical life?

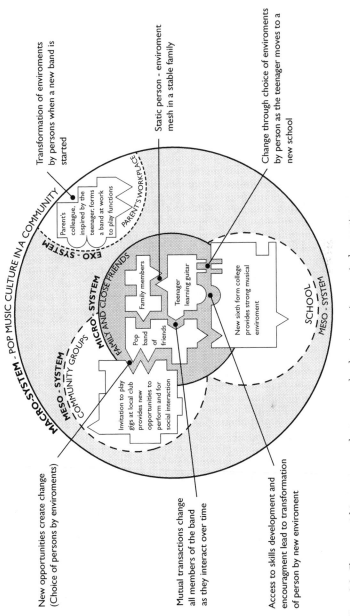

Figure 3.3 Changes within systems as the teenager develops increasing musical expertise

Transformation of enviroments by persons when a new band is started

Static person - enviroment mesh in a stable family

Change through choice of enviroments by person as the teenager moves to a new school

MACRO-SYSTEM - POP MUSIC CULTURE IN A COMMUNITY

EXO-SYSTEM

PARENT'S WORKPLACE

Parent's colleague, inspired by the teenager, forms a band at work to play functions

MESO - SYSTEM
COMMUNITY GROUPS

MICRO-SYSTEM

FAMILY AND CLOSE FRIENDS

Family members

Teenager learning guitar

Pop band of friends

New sixth form college provides strong enviroment

SCHOOL
MESO - SYSTEM

Invitation to play gigs at local club provides new opportunities to perform and for social interaction

New opportunities create change (Choice of persons by enviroments)

Mutual transactions change all members of the band as they interact over time

Access to skills development and encouragment lead to transformation of person by new enviroment

Prenatal auditory experiences of music

Although we are not aware of them, all of our sensory systems begin to function before birth. However, our responses to sound appear to be the most important. The information received through sound is more diverse and carries more information than the other senses, although it is muffled.[7] In the womb, we are exposed to our mother's voice, breathing, heartbeat, digestive system, body movements and footsteps. We also have information about the physical and emotional state of our mother. After twenty-eight to thirty weeks of gestation, we reliably react to external sounds. Where we have an enriched auditory environment, our aural perception is enhanced. As infants, we recognise music that we have heard in the womb both before and immediately after birth. We are more attentive to and soothed by music that our mothers have listened to daily in the last three months of pregnancy. This means that our musical enculturation, or lack of it, begins before we are born, although a small number of unborn children may experience amusia or be deaf which will limit their musical development.[7]

The development of musical perception in infancy and childhood

The impact of the home environment continues to be of great importance throughout our childhood. As infants, we are highly effective listeners and very sensitive to patterns of sounds that adults perceive as musical.[8] As soon as we are exposed to music, the skills required for understanding and analysing it start to develop. Typically, we develop a wide range of schemata for music from the pre-verbal quasi-musical interactions which we have with those caring for us. Bonding with our primary caregiver plays a crucial role in this two-way process. Each is, to some extent, sensitive to the physical and emotional state of the other. Those caring for us typically engage in infant-directed speech, known as motherese or parentese. This includes the adoption of a higher pitch of speech, a large dynamic range and regularity in the rhythm.[8] It is easy to identify this if you observe infant adult inter-actions. When the caregiver pauses in this speech, infants sometimes respond by making sounds or changing behaviour. Caregivers may interpret this as a form of conversation and respond, positively rein-forcing the behaviour. This type of infant-directed speech is similar across different cultures.

Caregivers in all parts of the world also sing to infants. This usually consists of lullabies, play songs or songs adapted from the adult rep-ertoire. Like infant-directed speech, singing is undertaken at a higher pitch and slower tempo than normal and the emotional aspects are exaggerated. Newborns and infants listen more attentively to this kind of singing than other forms.[8] Lullabies, across the world have common characteristics. They have smooth melodic contours with strong tonality, repetitive rhythms and a distinct vocal style. Infants prefer lullabies to all other songs. Singing, particularly by mothers, has a powerful impact on arousal levels. Lullabies sooth and encour-age sleep, while play songs lead to alert attention. Caregivers tend to instinctively adapt their behaviour to their child's needs. Gradually, as the child ages, caregivers adapt their singing style, lowering the pitch and more clearly articulating the lyrics as language skills develop. Ini-tially, infants are adept at perceiving music from other cultures as well as their own, but this changes over time as they become encultured into the tonal system of their culture.

The musical activities initiated by parents and the musical resources available to them in the home vary widely. The kind of music to which the child is exposed will depend on parental preferences. Parents may listen to very different genres, for instance, jazz, grunge, hip hop, classical music. Some may never listen to music or have it playing the background. Some homes provide opportunities for trying out musi-cal instruments. These different possibilities influence enculturation, the kind of musical schemata which are acquired and lead to disparate musical development. Consider how the musical environment of your home might have influenced your musical development. What kinds of activities did you engage in with your caregivers? What kind of music was played?

The development of pitch, melody and tonality

The way that infants group pitch sounds follows the same rules as adults. Tone sequences are grouped on the basis of similarities in pitch, loudness and timbre, although infants require greater differences than adults to notice change. Infants have sophisticated processing systems. They are able to identify sounds of the same pitch with a different harmonic structure, match pitches of vowels sung to them, discriminate changes in pitch as small as a semitone, recognise the direction of pitch change and distinguish tones an octave apart.[9] By six months old they can recognise differences in melodic contour and recognise melodies as the same even when they are presented at different pitch and tempo. Unlike adults they can detect changes to melodies when they are based in non-Western tonalities or invented scales as long as the intervals are similar to those in Western scales. They gradually become able to recognise differences in harmony and conventional musical endings in Western music endings on the tonic.[9]

Our ability to recognise pitch and contour seems to be innate and develops rapidly. In contrast, developing knowledge of the tonality of our culture takes time, in the same way as it takes time to learn our native language. As it is possible to be bilingual, it is possible to be bi-musical. The infant just needs to be exposed to two different musical systems. In Western cultures, after about a year of exposure to music, initial understanding of tonality develops. At some point between the age of four and seven years, children can generally organise songs around stable tonal keys, although they cannot transpose melodies. This develops later. Musical training accelerates the development of understanding of pitch and tonality, but does not change it radically.[9]

The development of the perception of rhythm

Infants have a predisposition for processing rhythm. Very young infants can detect small changes in tempo and, in some circumstances, can adapt their spontaneous sucking rate to a pulse. Newborns are sensitive to the beat in simple metric sequences and as early as four to eight months, infants develop preferences for metrical structures that are common in their culture.

Babies experience movement through being held, rocked and bounced and by about six months sway and bounce rhythmically in response to music. The extent to which they can co-ordinate with the music gradually increases with age. Early on, they are able to detect timing changes in music from other cultures but with greater exposure to music from their own culture, they soon experience adult like difficulties with complex metric structures which are unfamiliar to them. The spontaneous singing of two-year-olds shows evidence of a beat and rhythmic subdivisions overlaid on it and by the age of five most children can produce a steady beat when supported by adult modelling. Overall, there is little difference between children in the early stages of elementary school and adult non-musicians in their processing of pulse, metre and rhythm.

As with the processing of pitch, the basic processing structures for pulse, metre and rhythm appear to be present at birth. With increasing exposure, the infant develops greater skill in processing the rhythmic structures of their culture. This parallels the development of spoken language, where newborns learn the language(s) to which they are exposed. While other languages can be learned in later life, acquiring them is more difficult and subtleties of pronunciation may never be totally mastered.

The development of the perception of harmony and timbre

There is considerable debate about whether infants respond more positively to consonant as opposed to dissonant sounds. Some have argued that preference for consonance simply reflects human preferences which have influenced the types of music which have developed over time. Others argue that preference for consonance only develops through exposure to it and increasing familiarity with it.

This may be the case as in some cultures, music is not consistently consonant. For instance, folk singers in rural Croatia commonly sing duets in parallel seconds which many brought up in Western cultures may find dissonant.[8]

The discrimination of timbre develops rapidly in childhood as children are exposed to different sounds,[10] although they experience difficulties when sounds are similar. Increased exposure to specific sounds enhances the ability to discriminate between them.

The development of the perception of structure and form

To be able to understand the structure of music depends on being able to detect similarities and differences and to remember what you have heard. While young infants can discriminate many differences relating to pitch and rhythm this does not mean that they can understand the structure of what they are hearing. While most adults can easily recognise simple musical structures, for instance, verse and chorus, analysing long complex pieces of music can be challenging, even for trained musicians.

Musical memory in infancy and the early years

Infants are able to remember songs and other music that they hear frequently. This is essential if they are to learn to sing songs themselves. Knowledge of the tonal system of the song provides the framework for memorisation. Early infant memories of music seem to be extremely specific. For instance, at about six months old, infants can remember the specific tempo and timbre of music that they know but they do not recognise the piece of music when it is played at a different speed or by different instruments. By the time that they attend pre-school, children can recognise familiar tunes across many different types of transformations, so more flexible musical representations do develop.

Singing in the early years and childhood

From about nine months old, infants begin to make spontaneous babbling or singing sounds which are different to speech. Depending on the extent to which they experience interactive musical experiences with a caregiver, many at around a year will start adding word-like sounds as their mother is singing a song, gradually singing longer sections until they can sing the song independently. After eighteen months, infants begin to spontaneously create recognisable songs, however, they have not yet developed strong schemata for tonality, so a very limited set of phrase contours are used. By the age of three, typically, they rely on the words of the song and can produce distinct pitches but there is no stability of the intervals between notes or tonal coherence. At four, the child still relies on the text of the song, but the reproduction of its melodic contour is improving in accuracy, although the whole still lacks coherence. By the age of five or six years most children are able to reproduce recognisable songs accurately and can also improvise and invent songs.[9] The specific ages at which these changes occur depend on the musical environment which the child is exposed to. Home background or activities in a nursery play a crucial role in the extent to which pre-school children engage in singing. Can you remember the first songs that you learned? Did you learn these at home, in nursery or elsewhere? What do you remember of other people's responses to your singing? What impact did these responses have on your perceptions of your musical ability?

The perception of musical emotion in infants and children

Infants can respond to emotional expressiveness in music. For instance, they are able to distinguish between lullabies sung by mothers to their infants (they prefer these), as opposed to lullabies sung without the infant present. It is not until early childhood that they begin to be able to distinguish between emotions represented in music, for instance, happiness or sadness. The actual age at which they do this varies. Take a moment to think about how you distinguish between different emotions in music. What aspects of the music guide your judgements? Can you recall when you first were able to identify these emotions in music? Typically, in Western cultures, adult perceptions of emotion in music rely mainly on the tempo and whether the music is in a major or minor key. These factors also underpin children's assessments. Typically, by elementary school age, children perform similarly to adults in recognising emotions in music, although the age at which this occurs depends on the extent of the child's exposure to music within and across genres and their general cognitive and emotional development. They can also attach other meanings to music, for instance, those which are associated with events in their lives, the birth of a sibling, the death of a favourite pet. They may associate a piece of music with feeling happy because they listened to it in the car when going on holiday.

The development of musical preferences

We all have preferences for certain styles or genres of music. Infants and very young children tend to prefer child-oriented music, for instance, lullabies and nursery rhymes, while young children generally tend to be open eared with no particular preference for specific genres.[11] It is as we move towards adolescence that our musical preferences become more constrained and are an important element in establishing our identity. How did you develop your musical preferences? Was adolescence an important time for this? Was the influence of friends important?

During the teenage years the music that we listen to can define who our friends are and the way that we dress and conduct our lives. Music is one of the ways that we present ourselves to others, although privately we may engage with a wide range of music. Throughout our lives, musical preferences are important in the formation of interpersonal relationships and group membership. As we saw in Chapter 1, music is used to enhance the bonds within groups and also to enable outsiders to recognise a particular group as belonging together. Music acts as a badge of identity that relates to other aspects of lifestyle determining in and out group identification.[12] Musical training plays a role in musical preferences, but other factors are also important. Our relationships, the way we live and our beliefs are all related to our musical preferences.[13] Socio-economic status and geographical location have a major influence on who is able to access music,[14] particularly live music. Those who have higher incomes are more able to regularly go to the opera, musicals and rock concerts.[15] This is further explored in Chapter 4.

There are several theories relating[16] to the specific ways that musical preferences develop. The first relates to familiarity. This suggests that the more frequently we are exposed to particular genres of music, the more we like them.[17] A variant of this theory proposes that liking increases and decreases with familiarity in an inverted U shape. As we become more familiar with a piece of music, our liking may decrease.[16] This process interacts with the complexity of the music. More complex music may sustain our interest for longer. Overall, familiarity accounts for much of the variation in our musical preferences, although preferences do change in the short and long term.[18] Have your musical preferences changed over time? If so, how have they changed? What influenced that change?

Musical development in the teenage years and adulthood

During secondary education, young people's exposure to and engagement with music varies widely. Some young people have no formal musical education, whereas others play several instruments and actively participate in a wide range of ensembles. This is partly dependent on the extent to which music education forms part of compulsory education. Even in cultures where music education is an important element of formal schooling for all children, it constitutes a relatively small proportion of time when a lifetime perspective is taken. As children we may learn to play an instrument or sing in an ensemble. Some of us may lose interest and cease playing. If we continue musical activities into adulthood, they may be disrupted by family and work commitments.[19] More time becomes available in retirement and we may wish to learn or relearn an instrument or sing with others, desiring to improve our skills and musicianship.[20] For some music is a 'serious' leisure activity[21] and they commit a great deal of time and effort to it (see Chapter 4). How would you define your engagement with music? Are you mainly a listener? If you participate in active music making how committed are you?

Much musical engagement involves the reproduction of music created by others, although increasingly, there has been an acknowledgement that every individual can be musically creative. For those of school age, composing and improvisation are now an integral part of some formal compulsory music curricula and there are increasingly opportunities in community projects for people of all ages to develop creative musical skills and evidence that even the oldest old, with no formal musical training, can compose songs.[20,22]

For most people, it is listening to music that constitutes their main engagement. Listening is a top leisure activity and allows us to increase our understanding of music.[23] Technology has changed the way that we listen to music making it easily accessible. We can control what, when and how we listen and refine our musical preferences.[12] Music enables us to reminisce, particularly in older age, when music may also have spiritual relevance.[24] As we age, we are more susceptible to the development of acquired amusia through brain damage. This can have an impact on participating in musical activities and learning from them. We may also face challenges in terms of deteriorating hearing, eyesight and speed of processing, although we typically develop compensatory strategies to mitigate such physical and cognitive constraints.[19]

How often do you listen to music? Try keeping a diary for a few days and keep track of how often you listen and what you listen to. What can this tell you about yourself?

Conclusions

As a species, human beings are pre-programmed to process music. The basic systems for processing music are in place at birth and develop in the early years taking account of the dominant tonal system. The particular musical developmental trajectory that each of us follows depends on the cultural and family environment within which we are brought up, the opportunities that we have, the choices that we make in relation to those opportunities and our level of commitment. These can and do change throughout the lifespan. While infants and young children prefer child-focused music, as they get older children tend to be open eared with no strong musical preferences. These tend to develop in adolescence and are related to identity and group membership. While preferences change over time, in the short and long term they tend to have links with age, gender, personality, musical training and identity. Preferences are also linked to familiarity and the complexity of the music. Musical development can continue throughout the lifespan into old age through active music making or listening.

4

Music in everyday life

The development of electronic media in the latter part of the 20th century revolutionised access to and the use of music in our everyday lives. In the Western world, music is in evidence in almost every aspect of our lives. Music is played in supermarkets, shopping precincts, restaurants, places of worship, schools, on the radio and television and through the medium of recordings. Music plays an important role in the theatre, TV, films, video, video games and advertising. It is available in a wide variety of formats, through smart phones, ipads and computers which can stream music on demand. These new technologies have changed the way that people are able to interact with music. Increasingly individuals are able to control their listening leading to highly personalised and complex patterns of everyday music usage.

The extent to which people engage with music in the developed world is reflected in the size of the music industry worldwide. In the USA and the UK, music is amongst the top economic generators of income. Listening to music is a key leisure activity for people of all ages but particularly for adolescents and senior citizens.[1] Prior to these developments, music was only accessible for most people if they made it themselves or attended religious or social events. In addition to the increased availability of music for listening, there are also greater opportunities for actively making music. Many more people of all ages now learn to play instruments or sing and participate in musical groups. Overall, there is extensive evidence of the key role that music plays in people's lives.[2]

Why we listen to music

While we might think of listening as a focused activity which has the intention of enhancing musical understanding and appreciation, in practice, we may listen to music for a range of reasons. This does not mean that we are not listening with full attention.[2] As we saw in Chapter 1, nowadays we can use music to manipulate our moods, arousal and feelings and create environments which can manipulate the ways that other people feel and behave. We can use music, amongst other things, to reduce stress, to overcome powerful emotions, to generate the right mood for going to a party, to reminisce or to stimulate concentration, overall, to promote our well-being (see also Chapter 5). As we saw in Chapter 3, it can also support the way that we present ourselves and promote our development as human beings.[3]

When we are teenagers we typically listen to a great deal of music. This helps to pass time, alleviate boredom, relieve tension and distract from worries. Sometimes teenagers use music as a vehicle to express anger by storming into their bedrooms and turning up the volume of their music to express their feelings. As we saw in Chapter 3, one of the functions of music for adolescents is identity formation and communication of that identity. Young people tend to make friends with those with similar musical tastes.[4] By engaging in social comparisons adolescents are able to portray their own peer groups more positively than other groups in their network and are thus able to sustain positive self-evaluations. Music facilitates this process. Of course, sometimes these identities may be viewed negatively by society more generally, for instance, those who engage with heavy metal, hip hop, goth or grunge. Anti-social songs can lead to anti-social thoughts and attitudes and in some cases, this can prime aggressive behaviours in vulnerable young people[5] and may have a negative impact on those who are denigrated. Music exploring negative emotions can exacerbate mental health issues[6] and the impact of this can be exaggerated through interactions with like-minded peers in music sub-cultures.

Music can have different meanings and purposes for young people in different cultures. Generally, music falls along two overarching dimensions, a contemplative or affect dimension (individual) and an intrapersonal, interpersonal/social dimension (collectivism). Adolescents in more collectivist societies use music to convey cultural identity more than those in individualistic societies. Cross culturally there seem to be common functions of music listening in adolescence: music playing in the background; focused listening; the expression of negative emotions; relating to other emotions; dancing; and related to friendship, family, politics, values and cultural identity.[7]

These functions are similar to those described by older listeners who also use listening and making music as an expression of their individuality and a way of defining themselves.

Listening to specific pieces of music can support the recall of events and experiences and the emotions associated with those experiences, for instance, remembering a concert we attended, or what we were listening to when we heard the outcome of a major examination or job interview. For older people, listening to music can provide a way of avoiding feelings of isolation or loneliness, being distracted from health problems, feeling uplifted physically and psychologically or feeling rejuvenated. Music can reduce anxiety and stress levels, increase the threshold for pain endurance, make people feel more positive about life and enable them to escape reality, stimulate the imagination and contribute to feelings of spirituality.[8]

When you are listening to music are you aware of the extent to which it is affecting you? Some listeners are acutely aware of how music can change as well as fit their moods. They are better able to access and implement strategies to regulate their moods choosing music to fit any situation and meet their own physical, psychological and social needs. Older people tend to fall into this group, while women are more likely to use music to regulate emotions and moods than men.[1] The extent to which people are able to control the type of music they are listening to is crucial in terms of its benefits.[2] When individuals are exposed to music that they do not like in contexts where they have no control they may be able to remove themselves from the situation, for instance, if they are shopping or in a restaurant. If that is not possible the music can cause extreme distress. Having a neighbour who plays music at a high volume at all hours, particularly music that is disliked can be very stressful and drive people to resort to legal measures, or even violence, to deal with the situation.

Music as a support for everyday activities

You probably listen to music when you are doing other things. Most people do. We listen to music when we are travelling, carrying out boring tasks both physical (e.g. housework) and mental (homework, routine work tasks) and in relation to physical activity itself. Music can act to distract us, energise us, facilitate entrainment (moving in time) and enhance meaning.[2]

Music accompanies travelling more often than any other activity. When we are driving, music can enhance our performance or have a detrimental effect. Which of these applies depends on the type of music, the context and our personal characteristics. If we listen to loud fast music, it may encourage us to drive more quickly but if we are tired it may help us to maintain our concentration. When travelling on public transport music isolates us from other travellers, passes the time and prepares us to be in the right mood for our activities when we reach our destination.[2]

We frequently play music when we are faced with relatively straightforward intellectual tasks, for instance, school children frequently play music when completing their homework. As with driving, the effect of the music will depend on a range of factors which interact together. Models have now been developed which enable the effects to be better understood. Figure 4.1 sets out such a model. Generally, studying is enhanced when calming, relaxing music is played, although if the task is boring more stimulating music may be required to maintain concentration. Tasks involving rote memorisation tend

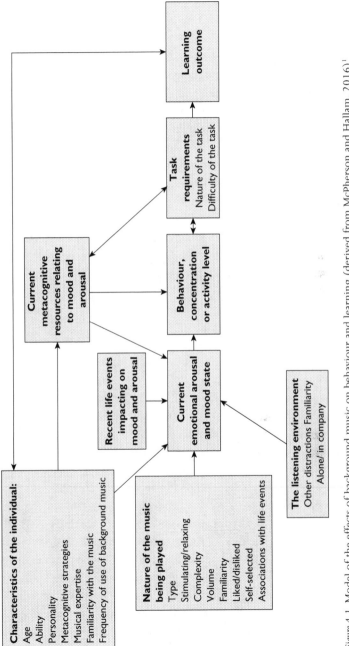

Figure 4.1 Model of the effects of background music on behaviour and learning (derived from McPherson and Hallam, 2016)[1]

to be particularly disrupted by music, although music can act as a mnemonic, for instance, a song commonly used to help children remember the alphabet. Where children have special educational needs which affect concentration, calming music can have positive effects on task performance.[9]

Music has always played a major part in work activities. It has been used to co-ordinate movement, alleviate boredom, develop team spirit and speed up the pace of work. Nowadays, singing to accompany work is much less common in the developed world but recorded music is played extensively in work places, shops, airports, restaurants and hotels. The commercial and industrial uses of music constitute major industries. In the office environment, those who listen to their own choice of music tend to maintain their focus when tasks are routine and solitary music can improve concentration, relieve boredom, reduce stress and block out unwanted noise.[2]

Music and leisure

The concept of leisure is not new. As long ago as the fourth century BCE, Aristotle referred to it as an active and embodied experience of melody, drama, poetry and dance. He conceived of these as 'noble' uses of leisure time and essential in supporting the happiness of citizens.[1] More recently, Stebbins[10] distinguishes between casual leisure which mainly includes social interactions and self-gratification behaviours which are fun and serious leisure which typically requires significant effort. Serious leisure participants can be amateurs, hobbyists or volunteers. Amateurs share similar expectations with professionals and rely on the general public to appreciate and support their activities typically through concert attendance. Music is a key element of their identity and they invest much time and energy in it. Hobbyists are similarly dedicated but there are no professional counterparts. Typically, their activities are undertaken alone. The terms hobbyist[10] or enthusiast[11] seem to best describe those whose focus is on listening and who have large collections of music, learn about and discuss music and acquire high quality equipment to play it. Some may be committed concert or festival goers. Volunteers offer help, either formally or informally at musical events. Dabblers or dilettantes participate in a leisure activity for a short time or to a limited degree.

If you are actively engaged in making music or listening to it on a regular basis how would you describe yourself in relation to these categories? Do they adequately describe your involvement? If not, why is this the case?

Listening to music as a leisure activity

Attending a live music event generally indicates a greater level of commitment to music than listening to recorded music. Typically, we attend live musical events to hear a particular artist or style of music, learn about new music, support or challenge our existing musical tastes or for personal and social reasons, for instance, going with friends or being part of a community.[12] Strong emotional responses to music most commonly occur in live settings. These tend to be enhanced if the performers appear to be enjoying the experience and if they interact with the audience. This transforms the experience from a passive to an active one. Music festivals offer unique opportunities for intense musical experiences. Physical proximity to the performers, social interactions and the music itself all make a contribution. The festival context can provide a sense of community and help support the development of identity, although there can be risks relating to the use of alcohol or drugs, overcrowding, other negative behaviours and public health issues. The sense of separation from everyday life tends to distinguish festivals from other musical experiences leading those attending to reflect on their lives and their understanding of themselves.[12]

Another interesting phenomenon is that of 'fandom'. Being a fan has variously been conceptualised as a symptom of social dysfunction, as a consumer strategy focused on pleasure and identity development, or wanting to develop interpersonal relationships with other music 'fans'.[1] Any, or all of these, may be applicable. To be a dedicated fan requires having sufficient finance to attend concerts and pay for recordings and, for the really dedicated, travel to distant performances. Higher incomes are required for this.[13]

The impact of socio-economic status and geographical location on engagement with cultural activities has been explored by the Audience Agency.[14] They identified ten distinct groups based on cultural values. These are set out here. As you read them see if you can identify yourself:

- Metroculturals (prosperous, liberal, urbanites interested in a very wide cultural spectrum);
- Commuterland culture buffs (affluent and professional consumers of culture);
- Experience seekers (highly active, diverse, social and ambitious, engaging with the arts on a regular basis);
- Dormitory dependables (from suburban and small towns with an interest in heritage activities and mainstream arts);
- Trips and treats (enjoy mainstream arts and popular culture influenced by children, family and friends);
- Home and heritage (from rural areas and small towns, engaging in daytime activities and historic events);
- Up our street (modest in habits and means with occasional engagement in popular arts, entertainment and museums);
- Facebook families (younger suburban and semi-urban who enjoy live music, eating out and popular entertainment such as pantomime);
- Kaleidoscope creativity (mix of backgrounds and ages, occasional visitors or participants, particularly in community-based events and festivals);
- Heydays (older, often limited by mobility to engage with arts and cultural events).

As with most categorisations, these may be over simplistic, but they highlight issues that people can face in relation to accessing live music related to finance and geographical location.

Relatively little attention has been given to understanding the behaviours of music enthusiasts and sound recording collectors.[11] They, mainly men, collect recordings to fulfil multiple motivational desires including emotional responses, the experience of being swept up in the music, the need to re-experience musical events or increase their knowledge of the field or to support their self-image.[15] Technological developments have led to further distinctions in terms of those who use technology, consume technology and have different downloading profiles (occasional downloaders, online listeners, explorer/ pioneers, the curious and duplicators).[16]

Making music as a leisure activity

In some cultures, music making is a central everyday activity. For instance, the Mekranoti Indians, primarily hunter gatherers, living in the Amazon rain forest in Brazil make music daily, the women singing for one to two hours in the morning and evening, the men singing very early each day (e.g. 4:30 AM), typically for two hours and also often for half an hour or so before sunset. While some of this activity, historically, may not have been related to leisure but the need for vigilance in case of attack, its continuation may be because active music making is intrinsically rewarding.[17] In Western cultures, we do not engage in everyday music making in this way.

Although listening to music may be the most common means of engagement with music, many people actively make music, learning to play instruments, playing in ensembles, singing in choirs and engaging in all kinds of informal music making. We make music with others because we love music, want to develop skills and respond to challenge and meet like-minded others. Music making is generally pleasurable and relaxing and provides opportunities for self-expression and the opportunity to demonstrate musical skills. It can give structure to life and offer opportunities to develop friendships, get relief from family and work pressures and provide spiritual fulfilment. Being a member of a musical group can also lead to feelings of belonging, trust and co-operation. Adult participation is frequently an extension of engagement with active music making in childhood in the home or at school, although the pattern of engagement seems to change over the life course, diminishing in the middle years and increasing in retirement. Life-changing events sometimes provide an impetus for re-engagement.

In the Western world the reasons for adult participation in music have been grouped into three broad categories:

- personal motivations (self-expression, recreation, self-improvement and use of leisure time);
- musical motivations (love of music, performing for oneself and others, learning more about music); and
- social motivations (meeting new people, being with friends and having a sense of belonging) and spirituality.

If you actively make music with others, do these categories and patterns of engagement reflect your experiences?

Music used to manipulate our emotions and behaviour

Have you tried turning the sound down when watching a film or drama on TV? What becomes apparent when you do so is that music creates atmosphere without which many scenes become meaningless. Probably the most famous example of the role of music in film is the shower scene in Psycho, which is disturbing without the music but so much more terrifying with it. Music contributes to our enjoyment of a film or TV programme in many ways.[18] Most movie music is designed to influence our emotions subconsciously. If the action is ambiguous the music can give us clues as to what is going on. When there is no other information music can help to define characters. Sometimes a character is given a theme. The meaning of such themes may vary depending on cultural differences, for instance, music that indicates bravery in one culture may indicate evil in another. Music is frequently more effective than dialogue in providing information to the audience, for instance, indicating the historical or future time period when the action is taking place. It can indicate urgency, building up tension when something frightening is going to happen, while increasing volume creates the impression of fast moving sequences. Where music accompanies actions, we remember the mood of the event better as the music deepens our emotional experience.[18]

How aware are you of the music in the environment when you are shopping, eating out or on the phone? Does music in these contexts irritate you or do you think it enhances your experience? Our shopping, eating and drinking habits can be manipulated through music. Did you know, for instance, that the speed at which we shop is positively related to the tempo and volume of any background music which is playing? When the music is slow, we spend longer shopping and consequently tend to spend more money. The type of music playing can influence what we buy. In one study, stereotypical French or German music was played in a supermarket. This influenced whether French or German wine was bought, although customers, who were interviewed later were unaware of the influence of the music. Similarly, a sound track depicting nature influenced the perceptions of the country of origin of orange juice, its cost, whether the oranges were genetically modified and beliefs about the health benefits of drinking it.[19] Music is used to encourage us to enter and browse in shops. It is selected to appeal to those likely to buy the range of products on offer. The effects of music used in this way depend on the match between the music and customer preferences, the familiarity of the music, the extent to which is liked and the customer's mood. Decisions about when to use music in retail environments are based on commercial value (sales, number of items purchased, rate of spending), affect (mood, arousal, pleasure) and duration (length of experience, time taken to serve customers, duration of music listening, time taken to make spending decisions). Overall, the evidence across a range of studies has shown that there are moderate effects of music on these.[20]

One of the ways that music is used commercially is to impact on our levels of arousal. For instance, restaurants can use music to change the speed at which we eat or drink. When slow music is playing, our speed of eating slows and we spend more money on drinks. Fast music increases speed of consumption. This can encourage faster turn round in busy periods. The type of music played when we are put on hold on the telephone can influence whether we hold or not. We are more likely to wait if we like the music.[19] As musical preferences vary widely across the population, businesses have difficult decisions to make about what kind of music they might play and whether it might drive some customers away. Some may decide that on balance it is better not to have any music playing.

In advertising, music plays a key role in encouraging us to buy particular products. It is perceived to enhance the attitudes of potential customers if it fits with or conforms to their conception of the nature of the product, for instance, exciting classical music is often used to advertise expensive sports cars. Food adverts tend to be accompanied by cheerful songs, which may include the product name in their lyrics. When music is well matched with the product, it is better remembered. Overall, music is effective in enhancing the appeal of products and promoting memory for them.[19]

As a general rule, we tend avoid music we do not like. This has led music to be used by the police or Local Authorities to persuade people they consider undesirable to move from public places. Typically, opera or other classical music is used for this purpose. The police have also used music to attempt to reduce aggressive behaviour in groups of people who have been drinking heavily by playing children's songs or other calming, pleasant music. Loud music has also been used as a form of psychological warfare. For instance, the United States military have played Metallica's 'Enter Sandman' at high volume for many hours at Guantanamo Bay and have used it as a form of torture. This has been formerly banned by the United Nations.

Conclusions

We listen to music for a range of reasons, to change our moods and emotions, to develop and maintain our identities and to support us as we carry out routine tasks. Listening to and making music are popular leisure activities for many people. Our level of commitment to these activities varies considerably. Attending concerts or festivals requires a greater level of interest than listening to recorded music but leads to similar benefits in terms of well-being as actively making music. Music is used in films to manipulate our emotions and commercially to encourage us to remember products, purchase them and influence our shopping, eating and on hold behaviour. When we have no control over the music we are hearing it can have serious detrimental effects.

5

The benefits of music to health and well-being

For centuries music has been viewed as having the potential to impact on our well-being. Socrates wrote:

> rhythm and harmony find their way into the inward places of the soul, on which they mightily fasten, imparting grace.[1]

Modern music therapy developed in the USA to support veterans with serious injuries returning from the second world war. Since then music therapists have worked with a broad range of people of all ages and music has been used to improve interpersonal relationships, enhance self-esteem and energise and organise behaviours through rhythm. Recently, there have been developments in what is known as music medicine, where music is used to promote good health and support patients in reducing anxiety and pain. Performing arts medicine has a similar focus with musicians going into hospitals to entertain and engage patients of all ages in music making to promote their recovery and psychological well-being following treatment. In addition to this there has been considerable interest in the way that music can promote well-being in everyday life as we actively make music or spend time listening to it. The boundaries between these different areas of work are blurred and change over time. For instance, work with Alzheimer sufferers in care homes was initiated by music therapists, but as its effectiveness was demonstrated and its practice spread, it has tended to be delivered by community musicians.

I have completed three reviews of the evidence relating to the wider benefits of music, the first in 2001 the last in 2014.[2,3,4] The amount of research undertaken has increased massively over this period. In this chapter, I will set out the overarching conclusions from this research with a few selected examples.

What do we mean by wellbeing?

If asked to do so, how would you define well-being? Currently, there are many definitions, although, broadly, well-being refers to how we feel about the quality of our lives including our emotional reactions and our overall level of satisfaction. Some definitions of well-being emphasise the eudaimonic aspects (positive human functioning) and others the hedonic (feeling good).[5] The emphasis given to each varies in different conceptualisations.

One popular approach to defining well-being, the needs satis-faction approach, refers to subjective well-being as reflecting the extent to which basic and universal human needs are met. These can be interpreted as including affection (being liked, loved, trusted, accepted); behavioural confirmation (doing things well, playing a useful role) and status (being respected, having recognised skills or qualities, being independent and autonomous).[6] An alternative approach is based on mirror images of the criteria for the most com-mon types of mental ill health, anxiety and depression.[5] This has been conceptualised as 'flourishing'. The ten categories of flourishing and the definitions of each are set out in Table 5.1.

Music and wellbeing

Table 5.2 sets out how musical activity might support flourishing. The elements relating to emotional stability, positive emotion and opti-mism have been grouped together as they all relate to music's impact

Table 5.1 Criteria for flourishing

Category	Criteria
Competence	Concentration, attention, decision making, general competence
Emotional stability	Feeling calm, relaxed, even tempered
Engagement	Interest, pleasure, enjoyment
Meaning	Purpose, worth, value in life
Optimism	Hopeful for the future
Positive emotion	Positive mood, happy, cheerful, contented
Positive relationships	Social relationships, positive affirmation
Resilience	Managing anxiety and worry, emotional resilience
Self-esteem	Feelings of self-worth, confidence
Vitality	Feeling energetic, not fatigued or lethargic

Table 5.2 How musical activity can support flourishing

Category	Evidence as to how engagement with music can meet these criteria
Competence	The development of musical skills and knowledge; benefits to aural perception and language skills, verbal memory, literacy, temporal-spatial reasoning, some elements of mathematics, intellectual development and attainment in children; benefits to seniors in terms of memory and reminiscence.
Emotional stability, positive emotion and optimism	Individuals use music to change moods and influence emotions. It has the potential to support emotional stability and optimism, and reduce anxiety.
Engagement	Music can provide enjoyment and pleasure across the lifespan and act as a motivator for those in difficult circumstances at any age
Meaning	Music can provide purpose in the lives of individuals across the lifespan and support the development of positive musical identities. For older people it may also include elements of spirituality.
Positive relationships	Actively making music usually requires social engagement with others. It can develop teamwork and opportunities for performance can provide positive feedback and social affirmation.

(Continued)

Table 5.2 Continued

Category	Evidence as to how engagement with music can meet these criteria
Resilience	Research with children and adults in challenging circumstances has shown that it can contribute to the development of resilience.
Self-esteem	Receiving positive feedback from performance or during learning activities can increase self-esteem throughout the lifespan.
Vitality	Music can energise and support physical activity through enhancing and maintaining motivation.

on our arousal levels, emotions and moods. The following sections provide examples of how music can support each of these aspects of flourishing. Although the examples are given under each heading, typically music has an impact on all simultaneously.

As you read through the following sections try to reflect on the impact that music may have had on you. Consider both its positive and negative impact. It is important to acknowledge that music contributes to well-being only insofar as it provides a positive experience. Where music is imposed by others and is not to our taste, or music making is not enjoyable and rewarding there are likely to be no positive effects and there may be negative ones (see Chapter 4).

Competence

When we actively engage in music making of any kind we develop musical skills. The types of skills developed and the extent to which they develop depend on the following: the nature of the activity, how much time commitment is made, the individual's learning skills and the nature and quality of the learning materials or tuition (see Chapter 7). In addition to musical competences, actively making music can enhance a range of other skills in young children relating to listening, concentration, memory, literacy, temporal-spatial reasoning (the ability to picture a spatial pattern and understand how items or pieces can fit into that space) and mathematics. For older children there may be benefits in terms of overall attainment, while older adults report enhanced concentration, attention and memory.[7,8] The benefits of music in relation to cognitive skills is considered in Chapter 8.

Emotional stability, positive emotion and optimism

As we saw in Chapter 4, in daily life, we use music to manage our moods and emotions. The impact of music on psychological well-being and good health is largely, although not exclusively, through the emotions it evokes. Music elicits emotions and changes moods through its stimulation of the autonomic nervous system. Bodily responses related to emotion include changes in dopamine, serotonin, cortisol, endorphin and oxytocin levels.[9] These can impact, without our conscious control, on a range of health outcomes. For instance, musical stimulation for babies born premature or underweight significantly reduces inconsolable crying as well as leading to improvement in a range of physiological measures including heart and respiration rates.[10] Those singing in choirs report benefits including physical relaxation and release of physical tension; emotional release and reduction of feelings of stress; a sense of happiness, positive mood, joy, elation and feeling high; and a sense of greater personal, emotional and physical well-being.[7] In hospitals musical activities help patients to relax and listening to familiar music can reduce anxiety, provide distraction and reduce stress during painful procedures. It may eliminate the need for sedation.[11,12]

Music making can help in controlling emotions. For instance, it can influence impulse control and self-regulation in young children and children with disabilities.[13,14] It can assist with managing anger, support the development of self-control and enable disaffected young people to express their emotions more effectively.[14] Unsurprisingly, drumming appears to be particularly effective in this respect.[4]

In vulnerable and older people musical activity can reduce depression, promote positive emotions, emotional regulation and provide spiritual experiences.[8,15] It can also support the healing of children who have been traumatised through war, those forced to fight, serve as spies, soldier-wives or camp followers and who are now refugees. Using their own cultural music and creative compositions can help these young people to overcome fears and difficulties and promote healing.[4]

Engagement

Young people who are disaffected can be re-engaged through music leading to improvement in school attendance and their attitudes towards school. Teenage boys respond well to drumming activities, in part because it reinforces their sense of masculinity, is fun and enhances positive values such as group cohesion, self-esteem along with behavioural and social competence.[16] Music can act as a vehicle for re-engaging those who are not in education, employment or training (NEETs). Learning to make music has been shown to enhance self-confidence, sense of achievement, motivation and aspirations, offer empowerment and support the development of friendships. Those participating also develop transferable skills, for instance, listening, reasoning, decision making, concentration, team working, time keeping, goal setting and meeting deadlines.[17]

Musical activities have also been used to enhance the confidence, communication and social skills of adult offenders.[18] Typically, participants are better able to reflect on their situation, believe that they can change and, in some cases, seek out opportunities for further education and training. For both young and adult offenders there are examples of substantial reductions in re-offending, although this is not always the case. Music seems to act as a hook to engage participants allowing the building of a trusting and non-judgemental relationship with the music facilitator. It is this that supports change.

Meaning

Music can give meaning and purpose to people across the lifespan. It can support the development of positive musical identities and strengthen individual and group identity in children and young people giving them a greater sense of purpose and self-confidence.[14,19] Adults who participate in active music making report that it is valued and worthwhile. For those in older age it can provide structure and purpose to daily living, enhancing motivation and reducing depression.[8]

Positive relationships

As we saw in Chapter 1, moving in time together promotes social bonding. This is important for the social development of infants as it promotes positive interactions with caregivers. Group music making, at any age, involves a strong element of socialising which contributes to feelings of belonging with out of school musical activities supporting the development of friendships with like-minded individuals, increased confidence and enhanced social networks. Overall, group music making supports children in improving their social and communication skills, co-operation and team work.[14]

Adults participating in musical groups report increased feelings of belonging, social adjustment, trust and co-operation and changes in relationships including reduced prejudice in communities which have been in conflict.[20] Making music with others requires teamwork, particularly when music is to be performed. Members of musical groups have to pay attention to the actions and intentions of the other players and their physical and emotional states. This is key to developing empathy, the ability to produce appropriate responses to others by identifying and taking account of their emotions, experiences and their likely responses. Musical participation increases empathy in children.[21]

Making music in groups can increase the acceptance of children with intellectual impairments and enhance young people's commitment to helping people in the community and working to correct social and economic inequalities.[22] Music therapy with autistic children contributes to improved social interaction and verbal and non-verbal communication.[23] Overall, making music with others develops bonds which are not easily created in other ways. It can lead participating individuals to become more tolerant and accepting of others.

Resilience

'Looked after children' in the UK have developed resilience in deal-
ing with the challenges that they face through engagement with
high quality music making. Their negotiation skills and co-operative
working improves, they learn to trust their peers, develop the capacity for self-expression and increased self- awareness, increase their
self-discipline, responsibility and sense of achievement and develop
positive relationships with adults.[24] Similarly, young people who
experience serious or multiple life stresses can increase their resilience following engagement in music programmes.[25]

Self-esteem

The beliefs that we hold about ourselves make a major contribution
to our sense of well-being. Positive self-beliefs depend on receiving
positive feedback from others and having supportive social relationships. Developing musical skills which are positively recognised by
family, friends and teachers can enhance self-concept across a range
of people, young and old.[4,8] The enhanced self-confidence which
arises from success in music can spill over into other areas, acting to
increase motivation and application.[4,14] However, if feedback from
others about musical participation is negative, this can have a detrimental effect on self-beliefs.

Music has been used in the criminal justice system with young and
adult offenders with a view to increasing self-esteem. The impact of
this is mediated by the extent to which the young people feel that
they own the music. This can present challenges as sometimes pre-
ferred music brings credibility and celebrity success with peers but
also the expression of criminal identity (genres associated with drugs,
guns, gangs, misogyny).[26]

Vitality

Music making can increase vitality. It provides opportunities to demonstrate existing skills and acquire new ones, can provide a structure

to life and offers opportunities to develop friendships, engage in social interaction, get relief from family and work pressures and provide spiritual fulfilment and pleasure.[8] Those involved in singing in choirs report a sense of happiness and positive moods, greater personal, emotional and physical well-being and an increased sense of arousal and energy.[7]

Benefits to physical health

In recent years there has been a greater recognition of the relationship between psychological and physical health and the way that mental health can impact on physical health. Music, with its impact on our moods, emotions and arousal levels has been shown to have benefits for our physical health, for instance, making and listening to music has a positive impact on the immune system.[9,27] Music can also have a more direct therapeutic role. For instance, it can support improvement in speech impairments following strokes,[28] support rehabilitation of motor movements in a range of conditions and improve the quality, range and speed of movements.[28] Music therapy also contributes to the treatment of a range of long-term psychiatric conditions including schizophrenia and depression.[29] Perceived health benefits identified by those singing in choirs include stress reduction, therapeutic benefit in relation to long-standing psychological and social problems; the exercising of the body through the physical exertion involved, especially the lungs and the disciplining of the skeletal-muscular system through the adoption of good posture.[30] Older choir participants have lower mortality rates, a lack of deterioration in physical health, with fewer visits to the doctor and less use of medication. Alzheimer patients can benefit from engagement with music as it encourages reminiscence and improves moods and behaviour, although it does not have any long-term impact on the underlying cognitive deterioration.[8]

Conclusions

Overall, there are many benefits to our well-being and physical health from engaging with music either through listening or actively making music. The benefits occur through the impact of music on our arousal levels, moods and emotions; the social aspects of group music making; the impact on our personal development; and in some cases directly through music therapy interventions. For the benefits of listening to be realised, the listener needs to like the music. Music imposed by others may not be to our taste and can create tension and distress. For the social and personal benefits to be realised, the quality of the interpersonal interactions between participants and those facilitating the musical activities is crucial. The quality of the teaching, the extent to which individuals experience success, and whether overall it is a positive experience contribute to whether there is a positive impact. If the musical experience is negative in any respect, then any possible positive effects will be marginal or non-existent.

6

Issues relating to musical ability

Introduction

There are no agreed definitions of what constitutes musical ability, or indeed the many different terms that have been used to refer to it (musical aptitude, musical potential, musical talent, musicality). Many people, as we shall see later, equate it with the ability to sing or play a musical instrument. Is this how you would define it? If you play an instrument, or sing regularly in a choir or other group, you may conceptualise it differently from someone who has no active, regular involvement in making music. Your definition may also be affected by your cultural background, views expressed in the media or by those in your social circle.

The origins of research on musical ability

During the latter part of the 19th century, psychologists became interested in the nature of human intelligence and set about devising tests to assess it, now commonly known as IQ tests. In parallel with this, some psychologists focused their attention on the nature of musical ability and how it might be measured. These early conceptualisations focused on aural perception, the capacity to hear differences in sound. For instance, in a typical musical ability test, individuals might be asked to identify differences in the pitch of individual notes, rhythmic and melodic patterns or how many notes were being played together. At this time, alongside beliefs about intelligence, many believed that musical ability was inherited and that this set a limit on the extent to which it might be enhanced through learning.

Historically, the purpose of such tests was to identify children who might benefit from having more intensive musical education, frequently instrumental lessons. Their aim was to assess aural discrimination skills with a view to predicting future musical outcomes. However, musical ability tests do not have a strong record in accurately predicting future musical outcomes as acquiring high-level musical skills requires considerable commitment and effort as we shall see in Chapter 7. Unsurprisingly, those who spend extensive amounts of time actively making music tend to improve their scores on the tests as their musical processing skills are enhanced. Despite this, musical ability tests continue to be used in some educational contexts.[1]

The evidence for the heritability of musical ability

As we saw in Chapter 1, there is general agreement that human beings as a species have the capacity for musical development, and that this capacity is as universal as linguistic ability.[2] Despite this, there is continuing controversy about the extent to which we differ in our capacity for developing musical skills and the extent to which this is determined by genetic factors. Early research on the genetic under-pinnings of musical ability focused on making comparisons of the measured musical ability between identical and fraternal twins and other family relationships. It was argued that if musical ability was determined by genes, identical twins should have very similar scores. The evidence from this research was mixed.[3]

Advances in research methods mean that it is now possible to explore the relationship between musical ability and specific genes. Studies with families in Finland have suggested that our musical perception is regulated by several genes, rather than a single gene.[4,5] While there do seem to be differences in our perceptual skills related to music, the extremes of these, extremely capable or incapable, are rare. Most of us demonstrate moderate perceptual abilities. This distribution is typical of a complex trait which is influenced by several underlying genes, environmental factors and the interactions between them. The evidence that the cerebral cortex has an amazing ability to respond to and re-organise in response to stimuli such as music supports this view. Current evidence suggests that musical training, when undertaken over extended periods of time, can potentially change brain functioning as well as brain structure.[6] As we saw in Chapter 2, the environment that we grow up in has a major impact on how we develop musically and brings about changes in the brain. Overall, interactions between genes and the environment provide a compelling explanation for individual differences in musical outcomes. The following sections consider examples.

Absolute pitch

People who have absolute pitch can identify or produce notes with no reference to other sounds. For instance, they may hear a noise made by a machine and be able to identify the pitch the machine is functioning at as a distinguishable musical note. Absolute pitch is rare in the general population (between 0.01% and 1%) and not common amongst professional musicians. Typically, only 4% to 8% of musicians possess it. Initially, there was an assumption that having absolute pitch was an all or nothing skill. However, we now know that there is variability in the extent to which it applies. For instance, some people are only able to identify pitches from the sounds of particular instruments, familiar sounds or within specific pitch ranges. This suggests that knowledge of absolute pitch is acquired incrementally over time as the result of ongoing experience, although there is also some support for it having a genetic basis as it is acquired quickly, without effort, tends to run in families, is present in autistic children and is found more frequently in people of East Asian ethnic decent.

It may be that as a species we are predisposed to attend to absolute pitch. For instance, when we are asked to sing a popular song, we typically sing at approximately the pitch level of the most common version of the song that we have heard. For more finely graded absolute pitch to develop, a particular gene combination and an appropriate environment at the right time seem to be needed, for instance, starting to play an instrument at an early age and exposure to teaching which emphasises consistent fixed tone associations, or playing a fixed pitch instrument, such as the piano.[7] There have been attempts to train people to acquire absolute pitch. Most of these attempts showed that children aged four to ten years improved but that the older children had more difficulty. The optimal time to develop these skills seems to be before the age of seven.[8]

Tone deafness (amusia)

Some of us experience difficulties in identifying differences in pitch. This is typically referred to as being tone-deaf. Tone deafness has been estimated to affect around 4% of the general population, although about 17% describe themselves as tone-deaf because they have difficulty in singing in tune. This may simply be because of a lack of exposure to music making. Unfortunately, not being able to sing in tune often leads people to believe that they are not 'musical', leading them to unnecessarily avoid making music with others. Hearing and producing pitch are not always inextricably linked, for instance, there are some tone-deaf individuals who cannot consciously perceive pitch differences smaller than a semitone, but who can produce these pitch intervals. Although tone-deaf individuals experience difficulty in discriminating pitch, they can usually detect changes in rhythm.[7]

Musical savants and children with Williams syndrome

In contrast to those who are tone-deaf, there are musical savants, whose general cognitive functioning is below normal levels but who exhibit high levels of musical ability. Many have absolute pitch. They are also sensitive to musical rules relating to harmony and the structure of musical compositions. Those who are autistic have enhanced skills for recognising patterns and find their detection highly rewarding.[9] While there is a clear underlying genetic basis for these skills, environmental influences are also important. Savants can develop skills in a range of areas, for instance, drawing, calculating calendar dates, mathematics and music. The skills developed depend on the stimuli available in the environment. Many musical savants have sight and language disorders, which may lead to increased development of auditory processing skills. Music can therefore become a focus of interest and its highly rule governed nature can act to reward engagement leading to repetition, which over time leads to the development of high levels of musical expertise. If musical opportunities are not present in the environment these skills will not develop.[10]

Children with Williams syndrome also have low measured intelligence. They experience difficulties with mathematical and spatial reasoning, but they are more adept than might be expected in language and musical skills providing that they have the right opportunities to develop them. They display greater emotional responses to music than most children, become interested at a younger age, spend more time listening to music and possess a highly sensitive emotional attachment to music. This gives them more incentive to engage with music.[2]

Musical prodigies

Musical prodigies display exceptional musical talent from an early age. Historical examples include Mozart, Bach, Beethoven and Mendelsshon. Approximately 1 in 47,000 children are considered to be prodigies.[10] One recent example is a six-year-old boy who had no formal musical tuition but, through copying others, could improvise his own musical pieces, sing in two languages, play numerous instruments and had high measured musical ability. These skills were acquired entirely through self-motivation.[11] Another musical prodigy, Alma Deutscher, began to play the piano at age two, the violin at age three and started composing at the age of four at which age she wrote her first opera about a pirate. She has given numerous concert performances, often of her own works and her opera, Cinderella, has been performed in various places around the world.

Musically gifted children tend to be particularly sensitive to the structure of music, its tonality, key, harmony and rhythm, and its expressive properties and can remember songs much earlier than other children. Whatever the underlying genetic makeup which facilitates these phenomena, appropriate environmental conditions have to be present. Parents and teachers have to be supportive and the child must be highly motivated in what has been described as a 'rage to master'.[12] Children with a genetic predisposition to develop high-level musical skills, whether prodigies, savants or Williams syndrome children, are similar in that their musical behaviours affect their interactions with others. If parents believe that their child has musical ability, they are likely to provide musical activities and reward engagement with them. This in turn encourages further musical activity, which supports skill development and the consequent changes in neural structures which serve as a scaffold for further development following training to produce outstanding musicians.

The challenge to the notion of inherited ability

Early research on musical ability tended to assume that it was inherited and fixed setting limits on what an individual could achieve. This notion has been challenged by the expertise paradigm which set out to explore what characterised expert performance in a range of different fields and how such expertise was acquired. As a result of this work a number of common characteristics have been identified across different fields.[13] The research revealed that experts excel mainly in their own areas of expertise with little transfer to other domains. For instance, being an expert in mathematics does not mean that you are good at languages. In music, even learning to perform in a different genre can be time consuming and difficult (see Chapter 7). One of the reasons for this is that as expertise develops many skills become automated. This means that they can be carried out without conscious thought freeing up capacity in the brain to focus on the current demands of the situation. For musicians, many aspects of performance are automated, including the technical aspects of their playing, reading notation or playing by ear. This enables them to focus on the particular performance that they are engaged with. When they learn new music, they are able to process groups of notes rather than individual notes and they work faster than novices. They have superior memory for music and operate at a deeper level than novices. Perhaps most importantly they develop strong self-monitoring skills, are aware of their own strengths and weaknesses and have a range of practising strategies available to them to best support learning and performance[14] (see Chapter 7 for more details).

Take a moment to think of an area where you have expertise. It might be related to your work, or perhaps a hobby, for instance, cooking, cycling, playing computer games. Can you identify which elements of your skill have become automated and which still require your conscious control? To what extent are you able to monitor progress towards your current goal? Are you able to identify your strengths and weaknesses and where you still want to improve?

The expertise paradigm challenges previously accepted notions that high-level achievement depends exclusively on inherited ability. It proposes that it is the time spent engaging in a particular activity which leads to the development of automaticity and high levels of skill development. In music, for instance, it has been established that classical Western musicians need to have accrued up to sixteen years of practice to achieve levels that will lead to international standing in playing an instrument. To achieve this requires starting at a very early age and, over succeeding years, increasing the amount of practice undertaken to as much as fifty hours a week by adolescence. While it is clear that to achieve high levels of musical expertise, we must spend a great deal of time engaging with music, there are substantial differences in the amount of time each of us needs to attain the same level. There are differences between instruments; typically, classical piano and stringed instruments require the greatest time investment. Those developing expertise in the classical tradition tend to face greater technical challenges which require more time to master than those in the field of popular music. A further issue is the quality of the practice and whether it is undertaken alone as a solitary activity or occurs as part of a group rehearsal. Aspiring musicians of any age vary in the effectiveness of their practising strategies, the extent to which they are able to manage their learning and their levels of concentration. Some adopt ineffective strategies and waste time in unproductive activities.[15] Different learning strategies are needed for different kinds of learning outcomes, for instance, memorising music, playing by ear, performing rehearsed music and sight reading. Generally, however, the greater the length of time spent on a particular activity the greater the skill level attained. For instance, if a learner spends time playing by ear and learning to improvise s/he will become very proficient at doing so. If the focus is on learning to read music s/he is likely to become a skilled sight reader. Musical skills are also acquired in other ways, for instance, through listening to music, engaging in playful musical activity and participating in group activities where learning and consolidation of skills occurs in an informal learning context.

Referring back to the area of expertise that you identified earlier consider how you acquired your skills over time? How much time did you spend? Did you make a deliberate effort to improve or did it just happen as you engaged with the activity?

Broadly, three phases of skills development have been proposed.[16] In the cognitive-verbal-motor stage learning is largely under our cognitive, conscious control. We have to understand what is required and carry it out while consciously providing self-instruction, or if we have a teacher s/he may prompt us. In the associative stage, we begin to put together a sequence of responses which become more fluent over time. We are able to detect when we are making mistakes and eliminate them. Feedback, in the case of music from the sounds produced, is important in supporting improvement. In the autonomous stage the skill becomes automated. We can carry it out without conscious effort. It will continue to improve each time it is used, becoming more fluent and quicker. In music we tend to acquire many skills simultaneously. New skills are constantly being added. As mastery of advanced skills is acquired, skills learned earlier are continuously practised and achieve greater automaticity. As one set of skills is becoming increasingly automated, others will be at the associative and cognitive stages. Can you identify these stages and how they might overlap in your chosen area of expertise?

The expertise paradigm is supported by neuroscientific research which has demonstrated the plasticity of the brain and how it continues to change throughout the lifespan. As we engage with different musical learning experiences over long periods of time permanent changes occur in the brain. The longer that we engage with music, the greater the neurological changes. Changes are specific to the particular musical learning undertaken; for instance, different parts of the brain respond to the processing of pitch in string players when compared with the complex memory for rhythm acquired by drummers. Overall, the brain responds by making changes based on our life experiences. It reflects our individual 'learning biography'.[17] In this way, once we actively engage with making music, our aural perception is enhanced and our scores on tests of musical ability improve.[3]

Recent conceptualisations of musical ability

As we have seen, early conceptions of musical ability focused on our ability to perceive differences in pitch, rhythm and melody. While perceptual skills are important in acquiring high-level musical skills, they are not sufficient on their own. This has led to different approaches to considering the nature of musical ability. One focus has been on sensitivity to the physical and emotional aspects of sound,[18] while another has focused on the ability to audiate (comprehend sound inwardly).[19] I and a colleague decided to explore what the general public, young people and a range of professionals believed constituted musical ability.[20] We found that when asked to complete the statement 'Musical ability is. . .' most respondents indicated that it was being able to play a musical instrument or sing. Is this how you would have completed the statement? Other respondents referred to a range of skills including listening and understanding, having an appreciation of music and being responsive to music, activities which most of us engage

in on a daily basis. In a follow up study, I created a series of state-
ments derived from the initial study and asked respondents to indicate their level of agreement with each statement.[21] About 600 people
completed the questionnaire. Musical ability was conceptualised in a
range of ways. Figure 6.1 sets out the average response in each area.
Overall, rhythm was given the highest ratings, which may reflect its
central role in much current popular music. Having a musical ear
ranked lower in responses than might have been expected given its
prominent position with regard to musical ability historically. High
ratings were given to motivation and personal commitment, demon-
strating their perceived importance in developing high-level skills.
The professional musicians who participated expressed the strongest
agreement that musical ability was related to communication, being

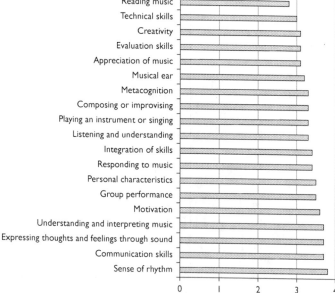

Perceptions of musical ability

Figure 6.1 Perceptions of Musical Ability

able to play in a group and emotional sensitivity indicating that these skills are crucial at the highest levels of performing expertise. Overall, the conceptions of musical ability generated from the research were complex and multi-faceted and reflected the wide range of expertise that is found in the music profession in the 21st century.

Another approach, which has taken account of the multi-faceted nature of musical expertise, has assessed musical sophistication.[22] An online survey of thousands of people identified five sub-areas:

- active musical engagement, how much time and financial resources are spent on music;
- self-reported perceptual abilities, accuracy of musical listening skills;
- musical training, amount of formal musical training received;
- self-reported singing abilities, accuracy of one's own singing; and
- sophisticated emotional engagement with music, ability to talk about the emotions that music expresses.

Analysis of the findings exploring the relationships between the sub-categories suggested that actively listening to music and deliberate aural processing could train some musical abilities in the absence of formal musical training as was discussed in Chapter 2. Younger participants reported higher levels of musically sophisticated behaviour, perhaps because of the increased availability of music in their lifetime compared with older participants. Musical sophistication was shown to develop early in life when there is more time and motivation to engage with music.

Over the last 100 years there have also been major changes in technology which have changed the nature of the music profession and the skills needed to be a member of it. While some musical careers are easily identified as requiring expert musical skills, for instance, performing, conducting, improvising, composing and teaching, there are others where the musical skills required are less obvious, for instance, instrument building and maintenance, music therapy, arts management, sound production, music publishing and work in libraries, broadcasting and journalism.[23] The internet has also changed the way that musicians, at any level of expertise, can make and create their own music and publicise it widely. Musicians not only need to acquire musical skills but many others if they are to have a career in music. Table 6.1 sets out the range of skills that musicians may need to develop. Some are applicable to all musical activities, others apply selectively to particular tasks, while some are related to non-musical activities, including social skills (being able to work with other musicians, promoters, the public); planning and organisational skills (planning practice schedules, programmes, travel arrangements) and time management skills (being punctual, meeting deadlines). These are clearly required for developing expertise in a range of professions and while necessary are not exclusively 'musical'.[24] To what extent do you think that you have expertise in relation to the skills set out in Table 6.1? Which are the most important to you?

Table 6.1 Skills that can be acquired in learning to play an instrument

Aural skills that support the development of:
- rhythmic accuracy and a sense of pulse;
- good intonation;
- the facility to know how music will sound without having to play it;
- playing by ear;
- improvisational skills.

Cognitive skills that support the development of:
- reading music;
- transposition;
- understanding keys;
- understanding harmony;
- understanding the structure of the music;
- the memorisation of music;
- composing;
- understanding different musical styles and their cultural and historic contexts.

Technical skills that support the development of:
- instrument specific skills;
- technical agility;
- articulation;
- expressive tone quality.

Musicianship skills that support the development of:
- expressive playing;
- sound projection;
- control;
- conveying musical meaning.

Performance skills that support the development of:
- communication with an audience;
- communication with other performers;
- being able to co-ordinate a group;
- presentation to an audience.

Creative skills that support the development of:
- interpretation;
- improvisation;
- composition.

Evaluative skills that support the development of:
- listening with understanding;
- being able to describe and discuss music;
- being able to make comparisons between different types of music and performances;
- critically assessing personal performance, improvisation and compositions;
- monitoring progress.

Self-regulatory skills that support the development of:
- managing the process of learning;
- managing practice;
- enhancing concentration;
- enhancing motivation.

Conclusions

There is general consensus that human beings as a species are pre-programmed to acquire a wide range of musical skills. Despite this, there continues to be debate about the extent to which genetic factors underpin or limit individual musical development. While tests of musical aptitude may assess an individual's current aural skills, to be successful in musical activities requires a wide range of different skills. While aural abilities are important, they do not provide the basis from which to accurately assess musical potential. Interest in music and opportunities to pursue those interests are crucial to enable us to develop our musical skills to their fullest extent and continue to engage with music in some capacity throughout our lives.

7

The development of specialist musical skills

As a species we have been engaged in making music for thousands of years. How we learned to play instruments and perform together at that time is not known but we do know that the first music schools were set up in Athens during the 6th and 5th centuries BCE where pupils aged between thirteen and sixteen were taught to play instruments and sing. Since then the most common approach to developing musical skills, at least in the Western world, has been through individual or small group lessons with expert teachers. More recently, technological developments have led to a wide range of opportunities for accessing and learning to make music informally.

The music profession is diverse. Musicians work in many musical cultures, in a wide range of genres and in different combinations. They may perform, improvise, compose or arrange music; contribute to its technological production; write about, analyse and critique music; and teach or facilitate music making in the community. The availability of software to support editing, notation, graphics-based composition, CD/DVD creation, video/podcast presentations, teaching and learning and interactive musical networking communities has enhanced the opportunities for musicians to diversify.[1] Most musicians now have what has become known as a portfolio career where they engage in many different types of musical activities in order to earn a living.

Historically, access to gaining high-level musical skills was limited to those who could afford to pay for lessons or learn through informal communities of practice, e.g. brass bands, folk groups, garage bands. Opportunities to learn to play a musical instrument throughout the lifespan have increased greatly in the Western world as societies have become more affluent as have opportunities to engage in a wide variety of amateur musical activities. Alongside this increase, the aims and aspirations of those actively making music have diversified. While some learners want to become professional musicians, many want amateur or hobbyist status (see Chapter 4). Despite this, learners of all ages want to achieve and gain musical skills while also enjoying making music. These aims are not mutually exclusive. Those facilitating musical activities can provide an environment which offers challenge and enjoyment, although there may be differences in content, for instance, repertoire, the emphasis on reading notation or improvisation. Whatever our aspirations, the most important set of skills which need to be developed are those which enable us to become independent and autonomous musical learners so that we can continue to learn when we cease to have expert support. Encouraging us to become independent learners requires that we think for ourselves, which means that we may question accepted practice. This can be uncomfortable for those teaching us.

The expertise paradigm

As we saw in Chapter 6, the expertise paradigm challenges the notion that high-level achievement depends on inherited ability. Its premise is that it is the length of time engaged in what has come to be known as 'deliberate' practice which is the best predictor of the level of expertise attained.[2] The evidence from neuroscience tends to support this. The longer we engage with musical learning, the greater the neurological changes that occur. These changes are specific to the particular musical learning undertaken. This is reflected in those attempting to learn to perform in a different genre. For instance, Sudnow,[3] a highly skilled, professional, classical musician, documented that it was extremely tedious, effortful, frustrating and time consuming to acquire expertise in jazz improvisation.

As we become more expert we are able to identify patterns. When reading musical notation, skilled readers do not fixate on each note, they fixate across line and phrase boundaries scanning ahead and returning to the current point of performance. They can continue to read about six or seven notes after removal of the printed page while poor readers only manage about three or four. As we become more expert we are able to learn and solve problems more quickly. We are better able to draw on knowledge stored in our long-term memory to facilitate current activity. The levels of automaticity that are developed in relation to skills frees up our working memory for other tasks. Expert musicians have well-developed metacognitive (awareness and understanding of one's own learning) and self-monitoring skills and can easily identify when they are making errors and generate new strategies to solve problems, while constantly monitoring and review-ing their progress.[4] However, the increasing levels of automaticity which we acquire as we become more expert in a particular field are not always advantageous. We can become over confident and overesti-mate our understanding of a problem. We can also become inflexible in our thinking, even in a creative field. High levels of automaticity can also make it difficult for us to access in detail how we actually do something. This can make it difficult for us to explain to others who have not yet acquired this skill. Think back to the skill that you identi-fied in Chapter 6. Have you tried to teach elements of this to anyone else? Was it difficult to explain how you do it?

When we develop expertise in any field we acquire executive, metacognitive strategies which are concerned with the planning, monitoring and evaluation of learning. They are crucial to all aspects of complex learning. In music, they can be considered at the level of a particular task or in relation to the more global concerns of the musician to maintain or improve the standard of their playing. In both cases knowledge of personal strengths and weaknesses, the nature of the task to be completed, possible strategies and the nature of the learning outcome are important. Typically, we develop our metacognitive skills as we progress from being a novice to acquiring greater levels of expertise. The more developed our metacognitive and self-regulatory skills the better we manage our environment and motivation to optimise learning. Returning to your chosen skill, to what extent are you able to manage the environment?

Musical practice

To attain even moderate levels of expertise in any field requires practice. To become a highly expert musician of any kind it is essential to practice. Take a moment to reflect on how much time you typically spend in your chosen area of expertise. Do you spend time specifically practising or have you gained your skills through the experience of undertaking the activity?

In music, those who have practised the most over long periods of time tend to attain higher levels of expertise than their peers. Those who develop international profiles as professional musicians tend to start learning at a very early age and accumulate many hours of practice while they are still young (see Chapter 6). While practice which has been accumulated over a long period of time tends to predict the level of expertise attained, time spent practising a specific piece of music is not a good predictor of its subsequent performance. One of the explanations for these differences is the quality of the practice undertaken, the more effective the practice the less time is needed to complete specific tasks. This issue has become particularly important in recent years as it has become clear that extensive physical practice can lead to long-term health problems for musicians. While mental practice (rehearsing mentally without contact with the instrument) can reduce the time spent in physical practice, it does not remove it entirely. This means that it is essential to develop effective practising strategies to reduce the time spent physically playing the instrument.

For practice to be effective and 'deliberate' it must be undertaken with the intention to improve.[2] Expert musicians, over time, develop effective strategies. When learning new repertoire, they establish the overall structure of the piece, ensure that they know what it should

sound like, identify difficult sections and work on them technically, gradually linking the sections together until the whole piece
is mastered. The sections are based on meaningful units relating to
the formal structure of the piece, its technical complexity and the
musical challenges. Further practice of small areas of difficulty may
continue up to the point of performance. They adopt a wide range of
detailed practice strategies to master technical issues, many of which
are related to specific instruments. A common one is playing slowly
to understand the complexity of a section and then gradually speed-
ing up.[5]

The practice of novices is not usually very effective. They often do
not have an aural conception of the piece that they are learning and
so are unable to recognise when they are making mistakes. They tend
to play through pieces rather than focusing on difficult sections, or
stop when they have made a mistake and return to the start. This is
counterproductive as they may never practise the later sections of the
piece. When they do realise that they have made a mistake they tend to
correct the single wrong note and carry on, or merely correct a small
section, perhaps half a bar. Initially, they tend to focus more on pitch
rather than rhythm. As their expertise develops they begin to be able
to recognise difficult sections and focus on these adopting a range of
strategies to master them and exhibit greater focus on interpretation
of the music in the same way as professionals.[6]

To improve, musicians rely on aural feedback from the sounds they
are producing. They constantly evaluate their progress in practice and
performance. They know what they are trying to achieve and monitor their progress against this ideal. In contrast, novices often do not
have a clear idea of what they are aiming for. In the initial stages of
learning, in particular, they are often reliant on teachers to provide
feedback. Nowadays, however, the easy availability of recorded music
and the ability to record oneself means that it is possible to monitor
progress more easily while also taking account of the perspective of
an audience.

For Western classical musicians, the time spent in practice tends
to increase as musical expertise develops as the repertoire becomes

longer and more demanding. But once professional status has been reached, as more time is spent in rehearsals with others and performances, individual practice declines. The amount of time spent in practice varies between instruments and genres. Classical pianists and string players tend to do most practice while classical singers tend to begin formal training later. This is in part because of the technical and repertoire demands of different instruments. Popular music tends to be less technically demanding, so less practice time may be required. Popular songs also tend to be short and relatively repetitive.

Practice is not always enjoyable. Even professional musicians may not enjoy practising, although they recognise that it is necessary. For instance, Nigel Kennedy, the internationally recognised violinist, reported in an interview that he watched quiz shows on the TV when carrying out routine exercises to maintain his technique as this kind of practice did not require intense concentration. Beginners often describe practice as boring or a chore and may engage in avoidance behaviours, for instance, taking time to maintain their instrument, finding music, putting up a music stand. They can easily become distracted. Those who practice infrequently tend to give up playing, while effective practisers are more likely to continue.

The development of creative skills

Learning to improvise within an established genre, for instance in jazz or baroque music, also requires practice. Initially, when learning to improvise, musicians may memorise short fragments that they have copied from recordings or developed through their own ideas. Gradually, they will be able to draw on these to develop their own style and improvise more freely. Learning to compose may evolve initially through improvisation, although this is not always the case.

Composition is usually viewed as requiring the highest levels of creativity, in part, because of its permanence in comparison with improvisation. The processes of composing are similar for children, young people and professional composers. While there is disagreement about the exact nature of the creative process, there is agreement that it is time consuming, both in the extensive period of training required to develop high-level skills and in the time taken in each creative act. The processes involved are typically the following: preparation (gathering of relevant information, assessment of the initial problem), incubation (time to mull over the problem, playful activities associated with it), illumination (flash of insight, derivation of a solution) and verification (formalisation and adaptation of the solution which may lead back to the preparation or incubation stages). Externally imposed constraints, the professional composer's commission and the instructions given to learners by teachers provide a framework. Such a framework is not only helpful but necessary, although a too-prescriptive framework can limit creativity.

Performing from memory

Professional classical musicians often have to perform lengthy pieces from memory. For many this is particularly anxiety provoking. Typically, by the time they have mastered the piece technically, musicians can remember most of it through aural (knowing the sound), kinaesthetic (movement) and visual memory (remembering where the notes are on the page). In relation to visual memory, there is an anecdote that a pianist, who in part relied on visual memory, during a concert stopped playing and requested that an audience member in the front row stop following the score as the page formation was different to the version she had learned and it was disrupting her performance. These automated, aural, kinaesthetic and visual memories are not secure and can break down in performance, particularly if the musician tries to think about what is coming next. This is because the memory coding is not available to conscious control. For memory to be secure, the musician needs to have a schema for the structure of the piece. Without this, in some forms of music, for instance, a rondo, which has a recurring main theme, without conscious knowledge of the order and exit points for each of the sub-themes the musician can keep repeating the music ad nauseum. Given these challenges you might question why musicians play without the music. The answer is partly that it is traditional, but also that communication with the audience is enhanced. Issues with musical memory are not restricted to classical musicians. Popular singers often experience difficulty recalling lyrics. For instance, Barbra Streisand, during a concert in New York's Central Park in 1967, forgot the lyrics to a song which led to her avoiding performing in public for nearly three decades. You Tube has many examples of similar memory lapses, for instance, Elvis, Miley Cyrus, Adele, Beyoncé and Mariah Carey.

Motivation and opportunity

Motivation plays a crucial role in the extent to which musical expertise is developed because of the high levels of commitment that are required. When young children engage with music, families are important in identifying the interest and potential of their children and supporting them, although in some parts of the world where making music is shared by all and an integral part of cultural rituals and everyday life, children share these activities and there tend to be no specific practices in place to identify those who may show a particular interest in music.[7] There are some exceptions to this, for instance, the Kaulong, an agrarian culture in Papua New Guinea, identify some children for special treatment and expect higher standards from these children, while the Wolof griots of Senegal identify some male children as particularly talented. They are then taken under the wing of a male relative and trained until sufficiently skilled to take part in public festivals.

In Western cultures, children and their families typically decide if and when a child will begin to play an instrument and what that instrument will be. Factors affecting instrument choice are complex and include availability, gender, parents' views, school or provider influences, friends, interests and enthusiasms. There are gender biases in instrument choice. Girls tend to prefer small, high-pitched instruments, while boys prefer those which are larger and lower pitched, although girls are less inhibited about selecting what is perceived as a more masculine instrument. Gender differences are also present in popular music with more girl vocalists and boy instrumentalists.

Overall, boys tend to predominate in playing electronic instruments and those relying on technology. If you play an instrument, just think about how you chose it? What influenced your decision? Did your choice have consequences for the way others perceived you?

Children differ in their motivation to engage with music. There are a range of reasons for these differences. Some relate to the children, in particular, the extent to which they love music and develop an identity where they perceive themselves as musicians. Music becomes part of the social life of some young people, they have friends who share this interest and they enjoy performing. They enjoy the challenges that music offers, have developed effective practising strategies and have positive self-beliefs about their musical abilities.[8] Typically, they have families who offer practical support and make resources available. Many will continue to engage with music throughout their lives in an amateur capacity, although some will go on to become professional musicians. Those who go on to become internationally recognised performers tend to begin playing when they are very young, have exceptionally dedicated parents who do everything they can to support the musical development of their child, sometimes at the expense of other children in the family and have very high expectations. They seek out the best teachers and ensure that their child benefits from every possible opportunity. The children themselves undertake many hours of practice and music becomes the focus of their life.

As teachers cannot learn for their learners and can only support learning, a huge part of their role is to engender a love of music and inspire their students. In the early stages of learning, they need to be relatively uncritical so that learning is fun. Later, when learners have made a commitment to music they want teachers to act as role models and provide ongoing critical feedback so that they can improve. Teacher-student relationships are critical in the extent to which students are motivated to continue to play an instrument. Motivation is enhanced if learners and teachers share similar aims. Particularly important is the repertoire to be learned, whether the focus is on musical outcomes, whether there is an emphasis on technique (scales, exercises) or taking examinations and whether the teacher encourages participation in ensembles so that friendships can be developed.

The success that the teacher has in engaging and working alongside parents is also important.[9] Because attitudes and emotions are learned alongside musical activities, teaching can have positive or negative consequences. For instance, the message that learners may take from their lessons is that music tuition is not enjoyable and that they are not good at music.

With the increase in technology, it is now much easier to learn to play an instrument without formal tuition. Learners can teach themselves, modelling their practice on recordings, on social media or deriving guidance from self-help tutors. They can join a community of practice where instrumental tuition is part of a wider musical experience, for instance, a folk group. They can engage in informal learning through combinations of trial and error, repetition, watching and taking advice from other players, reading and listening. Recently, there are many opportunities to learn instruments using a variety of computer software, through the web, or other interactive technology.

Not everyone who begins to learn an instrument continues to do so. There are many reasons for this. They may enjoy non-musical activities more, find that the time commitment to make progress is too great, dislike practice, lack self-belief in their musical potential, lack a musical identity or musical social life, dislike performing, experience negative peer pressure, have unsupportive parents or have insufficient financial resources to continue. Overall, a range of complex, interacting factors determine motivation to play and continue to play an instrument.[10] Some people regret giving up playing an instrument and take it up again in later life.

What has been important for you in maintaining your interest in your chosen area of expertise? Have you tried other activities and not continued with them? If so why was this? To what extent do your experiences reflect those outlined previously?

Performance

Performance plays a major part in the lives of musicians, whether they are amateurs or professionals, and they spend many hours preparing for it. Professional musicians recognise that the key element to successful performance is communication with the audience.[11] They know that their preparations need to be sufficiently thorough to ensure that technical elements of their playing are totally secure so that they can focus on the music and its interpretation. The movements that musicians make play a key role in communicating musical meaning and they may exaggerate these to support communication.[12]

A challenge for all musicians is performance anxiety. For classical musicians, technical challenges in music have increased over time and audiences expect live performances to be at the same high standard as recordings. Musicians are also under constant scrutiny from critics. The quality of performance at any given point is affected by the performer's level of expertise and adequacy of preparation, but can also be affected by psychological factors, such as self-beliefs. Performance anxiety is not restricted to classical musicians, for instance, Carly Simon abandoned the stage for seven years after collapsing from nerves before a concert in Pittsburgh in 1981 and the singer Donny Osmond had panic attacks during performances for a number of years.

There are many physiological symptoms of anxiety. Performers can experience increases in heart rate and respiration, tension in bodily muscles, 'butterflies' in the stomach, dry mouth, sweaty palms, cold hands, tremors, a frequent need to urinate, release of hormones such as adrenaline (epinephrine) and cortisol and gastrointestinal disturbances.[13] Do you recognise these from performances that you have given, musical or otherwise? Trembling and shaky hands, quivering voice, moistening lips and respiration are involved in the playing of many instruments and can have a direct impact on performance. Anxiety can also lead to a loss of concentration and attention and memory failure. However, being nervous can have beneficial effects. It prepares the body for the demands of the forthcoming task and increases motivation and concentration, particularly in experienced performers. It is important to differentiate between maladaptive (or debilitating) and adaptive (or facilitating) forms of musical performance anxiety.

Performance anxiety for any individual varies depending on interactions between the following:

- the performer's susceptibility to experiencing anxiety (this may depend on gender, age, general levels of anxiety, general self-beliefs and those specific to the particular performance);
- the likelihood of the music being performed well (this relates to the process of preparation, the task difficulty and the value place on it and anxiety coping strategies); and
- the characteristics of the specific environment in which the individual is expected to perform (influenced by audience presence, degree of exposure and venue characteristics).[13]

Most musicians develop strategies to cope with performance anxiety. They focus on maintaining a positive attitude and on reducing the perceived high stakes nature of the performance. For example, physiological arousal can be controlled by the acquisition of relaxation strategies; cognitive anxiety can be reduced by positive self-statements (I am well prepared) and the interruption of negative thoughts; and the anxiety-inducing potential of the task itself can be reduced by an appropriate choice of repertoire which realistically matches the performer's skill level. More generally, musicians can ensure that they are physically healthy and lead a lifestyle which will not increase their stress levels. Figure 7.1 sets out a time line relating to performance and its preparation.

Physiological demands of instrumental learning

Performance is often technically very demanding. As a result, in addition to psychological stress, it can generate physical stress. Physical and musculoskeletal damage can occur as a result of the repetitive use of the same muscles or maintaining bad posture during long hours of practice. This has led to some musicians no longer being able to perform. There is now an increased awareness of this issue

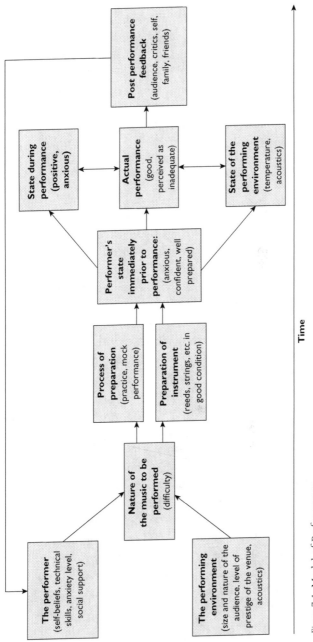

Figure 7.1 Model of Performance

and organisations which train professional musicians have begun to put in place measures to support young musicians in avoiding such injuries. Professional musicians are also exposed to a range of stresses and need to learn to cope with them including noise, unusual work schedules, poor lighting and environmental conditions and extensive travelling. Music-medicine specialists suggest that those training to be professional musicians need to consider how they practice, develop preventative physiological strategies and in general promote their good health.[14]

Conclusions

The processes underpinning the development of high levels of musical expertise are universal and apply across all cultures. All require time, effort and commitment, although the extent to which these are needed depends on the nature of the music itself and the cultural traditions which pertain in relation to the creation and performance of music. To maintain commitment, young musicians need to have a love of music, a positive musical identity, positive self-beliefs, a musical social life, enjoy performing and receive support from friends, parents and teachers. Those reaching the highest levels tend to begin to learn at a very early age and undertake many hours of practice. While practice has been shown to be important there is not a perfect relationship between the amount of practice undertaken and the level of expertise attained as the quality of practice is important. This tends to become more effective as expertise develops. Those engaging in creative musical activities, similarly, develop their expertise over long periods of time and expend considerable effort in doing so.

There are very great pressures on professional musicians. Performance is evaluated by audiences and critics and live performances are assessed in real time and compared with recordings. These conditions place considerable psychological and physiological demands on musicians. Those aspiring to be professional musicians need to be aware of these and take steps to ensure their own physical and psychological well-being.

8

The benefits of music to intellectual functioning

There has been considerable research considering the impact of actively making music on intellectual functioning. It has been undertaken adopting a wide range of research methods. Early research tended to explore the relationships between music abilities and other intellectual skills, for instance, music and mathematics. Comparisons have also been made between those identified as musicians and non-musicians. The difficulty with these research methods is that they cannot demonstrate causality. This can be explored through experimental intervention studies where the performance of those participating in musical activities, for instance in mathematics, is compared with the performance of those not participating. However, experimental interventions vary in length, the range of measures adopted to assess outcomes and the ages of the participants. This can lead to conflicting evidence. Qualitative research, including interviews, focus groups, ethnographic and case studies, can offer insights into the experiences of those involved but again cannot establish causality.

Recent research in neuroscience has been particularly important in identifying the way that the cerebral cortex self-organises in response to external stimuli and the learning activities that we engage in. Active engagement with music has a significant impact on brain structure and function. The changes reflect what has been learned and how it has been learned and influence the extent to which developed skills are able to transfer to other activities. The transfer of learning from one domain to another depends on the similarities between the processes involved. Some musical skills are more likely to transfer automatically than others. These include the perceptual processing of sound, the development of fine motor skills, emotional sensitivity, conceptions of the relationships between written materials and sound and the memorisation of extended information. Other benefits to intellectual functioning may relate to more general skills, for instance, self-regulation, persistence. This chapter provides a brief summary of the impact of music making on intellectual skills synthesising the findings from these different research traditions.[1] Before we consider the evidence, take a moment to reflect on your own musical activities. What, if any, intellectual benefits do you think you have derived from musical participation? As you read the chapter, consider to what extent the findings reflect your own experiences.

Aural perception and language skills

As we saw in Chapter 2, the processing of speech and music occurs automatically and there are close links between them. While there is ongoing debate about the exact nature of the relationship, it is clear that those who engage with music making in early childhood have enhanced neural development which has an impact on the processing of language. These changes can occur very quickly, as soon as eight weeks after beginning musical activity.[2]

Musicians of all ages process pitch and rhythmic information and emotions in the voice more effectively than non-musicians. The extent to which they can do this is related to the amount of musical training and its nature.[3] These enhanced perceptual skills play a role in the development of language.[4] Musicians are better able to perceive speech when it is accompanied by noise or is difficult to hear and are more proficient in making judgements about grammar, correctly pronouncing irregularly spelled words and remembering lyrics and short excerpts of speech. They have a larger vocabulary and in some cases, demonstrate greater understanding of complicated passages of text.[1]

Young children and those of school age who have musical training show enhanced neural development in relation to sound processing and are better able to discriminate between and concentrate on sound stimuli.[5] In one study, thirty-two eight-year-old children were assigned to music or painting training for six months. After musical but not painting training, children showed enhanced speech pitch discrimination abilities. Six months of musical training influenced the development of neural processes showing that relatively short periods of musical training had strong consequences for function and an increased sensitivity to linguistic pitch processing.[6] Overall, those who actively engage in music making are better at processing speech sounds and have greater phonological awareness (the specific ability to focus on and manipulate individual sounds, phonemes, in spoken words) than those who do not participate. The earlier the exposure to active music making and the greater the length of participation the greater the impact. Transfer of these skills is automatic and there is now accumulating evidence that this contributes not only to language development but also to literacy.[7]

The development of literacy skills

Phonological awareness is an important precursor to early reading and supports the decoding of words. It is strongly associated with auditory skills. Understanding text requires basic word decoding skills as well as higher-level cognitive processes such as memory and attention. There are demonstrable relationships between musical activity and various literacy skills including verbal and auditory working memory. Despite this, the evidence relating to reading per se has had mixed results. Some research shows strong evidence of the impact of music while some does not. This may be because music has not been the central focus of all programmes, some have been more general arts programmes. Where intervention studies have been highly controlled, there has generally been a positive impact on reading.[8] Differences in outcomes can also be explained by the type of musical training and the different ages and reading levels of the participating children. If children are already proficient readers, then musical interventions will have limited or no impact. When learning to read, phonological skill may be important initially, enhanced with short periods of musical engagement, whereas longer training may be needed to influence decoding, although some research shows improved reading comprehension but not decoding.[9]

Children who are experiencing problems with reading have been shown to benefit from musical participation, particularly when it is focused on rhythm. Rhythmic entrainment (being able to synchronise movement to an external rhythm) seems to be particularly important in supporting the learning and development of executive functions which play an important role in reading.[10] These are considered later in this chapter.

Where musical activities involve learning to read notation there may be a direct transfer to reading text. Singing, as it involves predictable text, segmenting words into syllables so that lyrics can be matched to music or recognising patterns, has been proposed as one possible explanation for the improvement of literacy following musical activity. Other possible explanations relate to changes in concentration and motivation brought about because of the intense and immediate focus required in music making and the persistence needed to improve performance.

While the precise nature of the relationship between musical training and reading skills are currently unclear there is sufficient accruing evidence to suggest that musical training which supports the development of pitch and rhythmic skills supports the development of more fluent reading leading to enhanced comprehension. Rhythmic training seems to be particularly important, especially for poor or dyslexic readers, who tend to experience difficulties in maintaining a pulse.

Aural and visual memory

Musical training can enhance auditory memory, not only for musical sounds and patterns but for prose passages, strings of digits, lists of words or non-words and short excerpts of speech.[11] Children who have musical training develop efficient memory strategies for

verbal materials. This may be because making music requires continued monitoring of meaningful chunks of information as individual
notes are combined into meaningful melodic phrases that have metric
structures which parallel stresses on syllables in language.

While musical training can enhance aural memory, the evidence
relating to visual memory is mixed. As music relies primarily on aural
processing, there is no particular reason why musicians should have
enhanced visual memory. Any impact on visual memory may depend
on the types of musical activity engaged with and the extent to which
they require the reading of notation.[1]

Spatial reasoning and mathematical performance

The relationship between music and spatial reasoning was brought
to the attention of the general public through the so-called Mozart
effect. This claimed that listening to ten minutes of Mozart enhanced
spatial reasoning, one element of IQ tests. Following this, CDs of
Mozart's music were produced specifically for playing to babies with
the claim that their intelligence would be enhanced. At this time,
I was involved in a live BBC TV programme, 'Tomorrow's World'
where more than 6,000 children, aged ten years old, either listened
to ten minutes of Mozart, the popular music groups Blur or Oasis or
me talking about psychological experiments. The children then completed two spatial reasoning tasks. Unsurprisingly, there was no statistical difference in the children's performance on the tests related to
what they listened to, although the children listening to the popular
music scored slightly higher, either because they enjoyed that music
more or because its lively nature increased their arousal levels and
concentration. Overall, listening to Mozart does not have an impact
on IQ, although it may create optimum arousal levels which can support concentration while undertaking specific tasks.

Research focusing on the impact of making music on temporal-
spatial reasoning has established that musicians have stronger spatial
abilities than non-musicians including mental rotation, visuo-spatial
search tasks and reaction times to a range of visual attention tasks. They

are better at matching a set of coloured blocks to a visual image, have better memory for line drawings and are more accurate when asked to mark the centre of a horizontal line, and to judge the orientation of a line. While this does not necessarily indicate that musical engagement enhanced these skills as they may already have been strong,[1] general music instruction, including singing, movement, playing percussion instruments or having piano lessons can assist children in the development of spatial ability. One review of fifteen studies[12] found a 'strong and reliable' relationship and concluded that music instruction led to dramatic improvements in performance on spatial-temporal measures. This review highlighted the consistency of the effects and likened them to differences of one inch in height or about eighty-four points on standard attainment tests. Early engagement with music making seemed to be important. Other reviews have also concluded that music instruction has consistent benefits for spatio-temporal reasoning skills.[13]

Historically, it was assumed that there was a strong connection between music and mathematics, in part, as musicians are constantly required to adopt quasi-mathematical processes to sub-divide beats and turn rhythmic notation into sound. However, the evidence for this is mixed and some of it is negative. Only very small relationships have been found between mathematics and musical skills,[14] while experimental studies with young children have been inconclusive.[15] One reason for this may be that musical training is associated with some aspects of mathematics but not others. Despite this, there has been some success in using music to consciously encourage the understanding of fractions.[1]

Intellectual development

Early studies focusing on the impact of musical engagement and intellectual development explored the relationships between the two. They did not address the direction of causality, leading some to argue that more intelligent children are drawn to participate in musical activities thus explaining the positive relationships. Indeed, there is evidence that children who take up a musical instrument frequently have higher-level academic skills prior to participating, although this is not always the case. As having instrumental lessons usually has a cost implication, take up is often related to the socio-economic status of families. Despite this, musicians, children and adults, tend to have enhanced intellectual skills, even when social economic status is taken into account although there are exceptions to this.[16]

The earliest interventionist research exploring the impact of music on intellectual development was undertaken in 1975. This found that children receiving Kodaly music lessons performed significantly higher than a control group on three of five sequencing tasks and four of five spatial tasks in an IQ test. No differences were found for verbal measures but the children in the experimental group had higher reading achievement scores which were maintained after two academic years.[17] In another carefully controlled study, children were randomly assigned to four different groups, two of which received music lessons (standard keyboard, Kodaly voice) for a year, while control groups received instruction in a non-musical artistic activity (drama) or no lessons. All four groups exhibited increases in IQ as would be expected over the time period, but the music groups had reliably larger increases. Children in the control groups had average increases of 4.3 points while the music groups had increases of 7 points. On all but two of the twelve subtests the music group had larger increases than the control groups. Notably, the music groups had larger increases on the four indexes that measured verbal ability, spatial ability, processing speed and attention.[18] While other studies support these findings, the impact is not always sustained after musical training ceases.[1] In addition, children who are more committed and spend longer making music tend to show the greatest change.[19]

A key issue arising from this research is the nature of the musical activity which brings about change. The musical interventions undertaken have been based on a variety of musical activities, some offering a broad musical education, others focused more closely on instrumental tuition. Currently, we do not know which, if any, specific musical activities are more beneficial, although it is clear that where the tuition is of poor quality, unstructured and with low expectations, there are no positive outcomes.

Executive functioning and self-regulation

One explanation for the impact of musical activities on intellectual skills draws on the mediating role of executive functioning and self-regulation. Executive functions are related to working memory (structures and processes used for temporarily storing and manipulating information) and involve the conscious control of action, thoughts, emotions and general abilities such as planning, the capacity to ignore irrelevant information, to inhibit incorrect automatic responses and to solve problems. Executive functions also include cognitive flexibility – the ability to adjust to novel or changing task demands. Executive functions are predominantly located in the frontal cortex.

Playing a musical instrument or singing, particularly in an ensemble, requires many sub-skills associated with executive functioning including sustained attention, goal-directed behaviour and cognitive flexibility. Formal music practice involves cognitive challenge, controlled attention for long periods of time, keeping musical passages in working memory or encoding them into long-term memory and decoding musical scores and translating them into motor programmes. These activities draw on complex cognitive functions which have been illustrated in brain imaging research.[1]

Studies of the relationships between active music making and enhanced executive functioning with adults have shown superiority in musicians of some executive functions when compared with non-musicians, for instance in non-verbal spatial tasks and auditory and visual colour naming tasks, visual attention, working memory, processing speed and ignoring irrelevant material. The frontal cortex of musicians, the area of the brain which is implicated in the regulation of attention, grey matter density, is enhanced in comparison with non-musicians and degeneration in this area is reduced for older music participants. Overall, active engagement in music making seems to prevent deterioration of the executive functions involving monitoring and planning.[20]

Undertaking musical practice on an instrument generally has a positive association with working memory capacity, processing speed and reasoning skills, although there are exceptions[1,21] in children and adolescents, even when parental education and participation in other school activities are taken into account. Those participating in musical activities have larger grey matter volume in the temporo-occipital and insular cortex. These changes in working memory are generally related to the number of hours spent in weekly practice. There is also evidence that music can enhance children's ability to ignore irrelevant information[22] and that this is positively related to changes in functional brain plasticity. While, overall, the jury is still out on the possible impact of music training on executive functions and their relationship with measured intelligence, it is clear that some elements of executive functioning are enhanced by musical training.

General attainment

Research exploring the relationship between participation in musical activities and attainment is generally based on considering the relationships between the two. This is problematic as there are many possible confounding factors including having supportive parents and a home environment conducive to studying. There is also the possibility that music programmes may attract students who are already amongst the highest attaining. Some research based on large datasets in the USA has shown that students who participate in musical activities tend to do better than their peers on many measures of academic achievement, although, overall the evidence is mixed in part due to methodological issues.[1] Working with an English Local Authority, I and a colleague examined academic progress in a range of academic subjects between the ages of eleven and sixteen and found that those who had learned to play an instrument did better at age sixteen than would have been expected on the basis of their attainment at age eleven. Those who had been playing for the longest period of time showed the most progress.[23]

Evidence from music programmes working with children in areas of high deprivation has also indicated a generally positive impact of participation on attainment. A recent review[23] concluded that the studies demonstrated significant and steady improvement with participants achieving targets and, sometimes but not always, out-performing comparison groups in mathematics, reading and writing.

Overall, children who experience musical training seem to have advantages in their school attainment even after general intelligence is controlled for. Motivation may be important as it is closely linked to aspirations and self-perceptions of ability. Active engagement with music can increase positive perceptions of self which may transfer to other areas of study and increase motivation to persist. Musical performances can involve trips to other places to perform, making new friends and broadening horizons and aspirations more generally.[24] Another possibility is that music students are more conscientious than non-music students. This would explain why they are more successful at school than would be indicated by their IQ scores,[25] although this too could be an outcome of developing regular, focused practice habits.

Overall, the evidence suggests a positive relationship between active music making and general attainment. What underpins this relationship is less clear. The relationship may be mediated by other factors, for instance, transfer of aural, phonemic, spatial and memory skills or those relating to planning, motivation or changed aspirations. Personality may also play a role. Western classical musicians tend to be introverts who are comfortable with the nature of solitary practice which in turn encourages autonomy and independence of thought. Musicians also score high on the traits of conscientiousness and openness to new experiences. The difficulty is establishing whether personality characteristics influence the take up and continuation of musical activities or whether the demands of making music influence personality development. It is most likely that there is an interaction between the two.[25]

Cognitive functioning in adults

The increase in the older population in much of the developed world has led to a focus on possible ways to maintain their health and well-being. Self-reports of older people who are engaged in actively making music include improvement in attention, concentration, memory, learning and processing speed.[26] For these benefits to be maintained musical activity must be continuous as there is a decline when activities cease. As we saw in Chapter 5, musical activity can relieve some symptoms of Alzheimer's disease. It can support the retrieval of long-term memories and enhance mood and behaviour.

Conclusions

Overall, there can be a range of benefits of active engagement in making music on intellectual skills. These include the following:

- aural perception, which in turn supports the development of language and literacy skills;
- enhanced aural memory skills;
- spatial reasoning which contributes to some elements of mathematics;
- the enhancement of measured intelligence;
- executive functioning which is implicated in intelligence and academic learning more generally;
- self-regulation which is implicated in all forms of learning requiring extensive practice; and
- academic attainment.

Currently, we do not know which musical activities are implicated in bringing about these changes, although we do know that they need to be of high quality. The greatest benefits occur when the activities are maintained over time, start early and are continued with high levels of commitment. To date, the impact of gender, genetic differences, for instance, tone deafness, and other individual differences on changes in the brain relating to musical activities have not been explored. The extent of musical experiences prior to formal training may also be important as we saw in Chapter 3. To maintain motivation, musical activities need to be highly interactive and offer opportunities for developing new skills, performing and receiving positive recognition and rewards. These apply whatever the age of the participants.

Further reading

You can see parrots moving to a beat at www.youtube.com/watch?v=6JSDxgHOJw

In the BBC programme *Tunes for tyrants*, Suzy Klein illustrates music's crucial role in the most turbulent years of the 20th century in Russia and Germany. www.bbc.co.uk/programmes/b097f5vs

You can see examples of protest songs at www.youtube.com/watch?v=nVhND8rzqh4

This YouTube site includes a wide range of very different football anthems from round the world. In general, they reflect the musical characteristics of the home country www.youtube.com/channel/UCo1zeq0zxJHdk9mhC3ucC3w

This site has a video of Luciano Pavarotti performing 'Nessun Dorma' at the 1990 FIFA world cup www.youtube.com/watch?v=V5moKfZ9Y2Q

A video of Elton John singing 'Candle in the Wind' at Princess Diana's funeral can be found at www.youtube.com/watch?v=DhQJUpThbZ4

The theme tune to the BBC Music while you work programme is available here. www.youtube.com/watch?v=RMEpjDFHN50

For a history of the psychology of music see Deutsch, D. Psychology of music, history, antiquity to the 19th century. *Grove Music Online, Oxford Music Online.* Oxford: Oxford University Press.

Daniel Levitin's book 'This is your brain on music' gives an easily readable account of how the brain perceives music and how composers exploit our reaction to musical material. He draws on examples from a wide range of musical genres to elucidate his ideas.

This site has examples of North Indian tala www.ancient-future.com/theka.html

This site has examples of many Indian raga www.allmusic.com/album/raga-guide-a-survey-of-74-hindustani-ragas-mw0000246246

This site provides an explanation of the Balinese slendro and pelog www.youtube.com/watch?v=3Ku9iH2pU9g

If you want to learn more about musical development, the following chapters are useful.

Trehub, S. E. (2016). Infant musicality. In S. Hallam, I. Cross, & M. Thaut. *Oxford handbook of psychology of music* (2nd edition, pp. 387–398). Oxford: Oxford University Press.

Lamont, A. (2016). Musical development from the early years onwards. In S. Hallam, I. Cross, & M. Thaut. *Oxford handbook of psychology of music* (2nd edition, pp. 399–414). Oxford: Oxford University Press.

For an example of motherese and an infant's response see www.youtube.com/watch?v=6KHZe0rr8q8

An example of a two year-old singing 'Old MacDonald had a farm' illustrating early singing can be found on www.youtube.com/watch?v=nuj2X2YeWn4.

The following website provides a list of different musical genres giving an indication of the current diversity in musical styles: www.musicgenreslist.com/

To learn more about music in everyday life, try the following chapter: Lamont, A., Greasley, A., & Sloboda, J. (2016) Choosing to hear music: Motivation, process and effect. In S. Hallam, I. Cross, & M. Thaut (eds.), *The oxford handbook of music psychology* (2nd edition, pp. 711–724). Oxford: Oxford University press.

For some examples of the way songs are used in advertising, see https://contently.com/strategist/2015.04/09/the-10-best-songs-in-advertising/

Examples of the role of music in cinema can be found in the BBC programme 'The sound of cinema: the music that made the movies'. Neil Brand explores the work of movie composers and demonstrates their techniques. www.bbc.co.uk/programmes/b03b51db

If you want to know more about music and well-being, try reading the following:

MacDonald, R., Kreutz, G., & Mitchell, L. (2012) *Music, health and wellbeing*. Oxford: Oxford University Press.

This video clip shows the impact of music on those suffering from dementia. www.youtube.com/watch?v=HsyGSA2-qVg

To see an example of a music therapy programme for children in Boston Children's Hospital go to www.bing.com/videos/search?q=you+tube+videos+music+in+hospitals+children+boston&view=detail&mid=AE1261832CD7D15E1485AE1261832CD7D15E1485&FORM=VIRE

If you are interested in issues relating to musical ability try reading Hallam, S. (2016) Musicality. In G. McPherson (ed.), *The child as musician: A handbook of musical development* (2nd edition, pp. 69–80). Oxford: Oxford University Press.

For video footage relating to the protegee Alma Deutscher, go to www.youtube.com/user/AlmaDeutscher

For an account of the life of Derek Paravicini a British musical savant, see Ockelford, A. (2008). *In the key of genius: The extraordinary life of Derek Paravicini*. London: Arrow.

For examples of Derek's playing, see www.youtube.com/user/derekparavicini

To download the musical sophistication questionnaire, go to www.gold.ac.uk/music-mind-brain/gold-msi/download

If you are interested in the development of specialist musical skills, try reading the following:

Hallam, S. (2012). Commentary. In G. McPherson, & G. Welch (eds.), *Oxford handbook of music education*. Oxford: Oxford University Press.

Hallam, S., & Bautista, A. (2012). Processes of instrumental learning: The development of musical expertise. In G. McPherson, & G. Welch (eds.), *Oxford handbook of music education*. Oxford: Oxford University Press.

Impett, J. (2016). Making a mark: The psychology of composition. In S. Hallam, I. Cross, & M. Thaut (eds.), *Oxford handbook of music psychology* (2nd edition, pp. 651–666). Oxford: Oxford University Press.

Ashley, R. (2016). Musical improvisation. In S. Hallam, I. Cross, & M. Thaut (eds.), *Oxford handbook of music psychology* (2nd edition, pp. 667–679). Oxford: Oxford University Press.

The following gives an account of the impact of technology on developing specialist music skills:

Webb, M., & Seddon, F. A. (2012). Musical instrument learning, music ensembles, and musicianship in a global and digital age. In G. E. McPherson, &

G. F. Welch (eds.), *The oxford handbook of music education, Volume 1* (pp 752–768).

For video footage of popular musicians forgetting lyrics, go to www.vh1.com/news/26000/musicians-forget-their-own-lyrics/

The documentary of a concert journey of the Berlin Philharmonic, *Trip to Asia* (Dirks, Grube, Thilo & Grube, 2008), gives an insight into the daily high level demands on classical orchestra musicians. www.youtube.com/watch?v=_GcQ3Jyu9Ek

If you are interested in the impact of music making on intellectual skills, the following offers a review:

Hallam, S. (2014). *The power of music: A research synthesis of the impact of actively making music on the intellectual, social and personal development of children and young people.* London: iMERC.

There are many examples of teaching using the Kodaly method on YouTube. This is one example: www.youtube.com/watch?v=vREbeqR4EtQ

References

Chapter 1

1 Jacobs, A. (1972). *New dictionary of music* (2nd edition). Harmondsworth: Penguin Books.

2 Sykes, J. B. (1983). *Concise Oxford dictionary* (7th edition). Oxford: University Press.

3 Gourlay, K. (1984). The non-universality of music and the universality of non-music. *The World of Music*, 26(2), 25–39.

4 Blacking, J. (1973). *How musical is man?* Seattle: University of Washington Press.

5 Cross, I., & Morley, I. (2009). The evolution of music: Theories, definitions and the nature of the evidence. In S. Malloch & C. Trevarthen (eds.), *Communicative musicality* (pp. 61–81). Oxford: Oxford University Press.

6 Tan, S-L., Pfordresher, P., & Harre, R. (2012). *Psychology of music: From sound to significance*. Hove and New York: Psychology Press/Taylor and Francis.

7 Levitin, D. J. (2008). *The world in six songs: How the musical brain created human nature*. New York: Dutton.

8 Schachner, A., Brady, T. F., Pepperberg, I., & Hauser, M. D. (2009). Spontaneous motor entrainment to music in multiple vocal mimicking species. *Current Biology*, 19(10), 831–836.

9 Gray, P. M., Krause, B., Atema, J., Payne, R., Krumhansl, C., & Baptista, L. (2001). The music of nature and the nature of music. *Science*, 5(1), 52–54.

10 Merker, B. (2009). Ritual foundations of human uniqueness. In S. Malloch & C. Trevarthen (eds.), *Communicative musicality*. Oxford: Oxford University Press.

11 Miller, G. (2000). Evolution of human music through sexual selection. In N. L. Wallin, B. Merker, & S. Brown (eds.), *The origins of music* (pp. 329–360). Cambridge, MA: The MIT Press.

12 Huron, D. (2003). Is music an evolutionary adaptation? In I. Peretz & R. Zatorre (eds.), *The cognitive neuroscience of music* (pp. 57–77). Oxford: Oxford University Press.

13 Brown, D. (1991). *Human universals*. New York: McGraw-Hill.

14 Cross, I. (2003). Music, cognition, culture and evolution. In I. Peretz & R. Zatorre (eds.), *The cognitive neuroscience of music* (pp. 42–56). Oxford: Oxford University Press.

15 Sperber, D. (1996). *Explaining culture*. Oxford: Blackwell.

16 Pinker, S. (1997). *How the mind works*. New York: W.W. Norton.

17 DeNora, T. (2000). *Music in everyday life*. Cambridge, MA: Cambridge University Press.

18 for a review see Hallam, S. (2014). *The power of music: A research synthesis of the impact of actively making music on the intellectual, social and personal development of children and young people*. London: iMERC.

19 Tan, Siu-Lan., Pfordresher, Peter., & Harré, Rom. (2010). *Psychology of music: From sound to significance*. New York: Psychology Press.

20 Thompson, W. F. (2014). *Music, thought, and feeling: Understanding the psychology of music* (2nd Edition). New York: Oxford University Press.

21 Deutsch, D. *Psychology of music, history, antiquity to the 19th century*. Grove Music Online, Oxford Music Online. Oxford University Press. Retrieved April 9, 2016.

Chapter 2

1 Levitin, D. (2006). *This is your brain on music*. London: Atlantic books.

2 For a review see Bigand, E., & Poulin-Charronnat, B. (2006). Are we "experienced listeners"? A review of the musical capacities that do not depend on formal musical training. *Cognition, 100*, 100–130.

3 For a review see Loui, P. (2016). Disorders of music cognition. In S. Hallam, I. Cross, & M. Thaut (eds.), *The Oxford handbook of music psychology* (pp. 307–324). Oxford: Oxford University Press.

4 Demorest, S. M., & Morrison, S. J. (2003). Exploring the influence of cultural familiarity and expertise on neurological responses to music. *Annals of the New York Academy of Sciences, 999*, 112–117.

5 Deutsch, D. (ed). (2013). *The psychology of music.* New York: Academic Press.

6 Large, E. W., & Snyder, J. S. (2009). Pulse and meter as neural resonance. *Annals of the New York Academy of Sciences,* 1169, 46–57.

7 For a review see Stainsby, T., & Cross, I. (2016). The perception of pitch. In S. Hallam, I. Cross, & M. Thaut (eds.), *The Oxford handbook of music psychology* (pp. 63–80). Oxford: Oxford University Press.

8 Lerdahl, F. (2001). *Tonal pitch space.* New York: Oxford University Press.

9 Bharucha, J. J. (1987). Music cognition and perceptual facilitation: A connectionist framework. *Music Perception,* 5(1), 1–30.

10 For a review see McAdams, S., & Giordano, B. L. (2016). The perception of musical timbre. In S. Hallam, I. Cross, & M. Thaut (eds.), *The Oxford handbook of music psychology* (pp. 113–123). Oxford: Oxford University Press.

11 For a review see Bigand, E., & Poulin-Charronnat, B. (2016). Tonal cognition. In S. Hallam, I. Cross, & M. Thaut (eds.), *The Oxford Handbook of Music Psychology* (pp. 95–112). Oxford: Oxford University Press.

12 Lerdahl, F., & Jackendoff, R. (1983). *A generative theory of tonal music.* Cambridge, MA: The MIT press.

13 Deliege, I., & Melen, M. (1997). Cue abstraction in the representation of music form. In I. Deliege & J. Sloboda (eds.), *Perception and cognition of music* (pp. 387–341). Hove: East Sussex: Psychology Press.

14 Williamson, V., Jilka, S., Fry, J., Finkel, S., Müllensiefen, D., & Stewart, L. (2012). How do earworms start? Classifying the everyday circumstances of involuntary musical imagery (Earworms). *Psychology of Music,* 40(3), 259–284.

15 Kellaris, J. J. (2001). Identifying properties of tunes that get 'stuck in your head. In *Proceedings of the Society for Consumer Psychology* (pp. 66–67). Scottsdale, AZ: American Psychological Society.

16 For a review see Huron, D. (2016). Aesthetics. In S. Hallam, I. Cross & M. Thaut (eds.), *The Oxford handbook of music psychology* (pp. 233–246). Oxford: Oxford University Press.

17 Brown, S. B., Gao, X., Tisdelle, L., Eickhoff, S. B., & Liotti, M. (2011). Naturalizing aesthetics: Brain areas for aesthetic appraisal across sensory modalities. *NeuroImage,* 58, 250–258.

18 For a review see Hallam, S., Creech, A., & Varvarigou, M. (2017). Well-being and music leisure activity through the lifespan: A psychological perspective. In R. Mantie & G. D. Smith (eds.), *Oxford handbook of music making and leisure* (pp. 31–60). Oxford: Oxford University Press.

19 For a review sese Gabrielsson, A. (2016). The relationship between musical structure and perceived expression. In S. Hallam, I. Cross, & M. Thaut (eds.), *The Oxford handbook of music psychology* (pp. 215–232). Oxford: Oxford University Press.

20 For a review see Juslin, P. N. (2016). Emotional responses to music. In S. Hallam, I. Cross, & M. Thaut (eds.), *The Oxford handbook of music psychology* (pp. 197–214). Oxford: Oxford University Press.

21 For a review see Hodges, D. A. (2016). The neuroaesthetics of music. In S. Hallam, I. Cross, & M. Thaut (eds.), *The Oxford handbook of music psychology* (pp. 247–262). Oxford: Oxford University Press.

22 For a review see Peretz, I. (2010). Towards a neurobiology of musical emotions. In P. Juslin & J. Sloboda (eds.), *Handbook of music and emotions* (pp. 99–126). Oxford: Oxford University Press.

23 Meyer, L. (1956). *Emotion and meaning in music*. Chicago: The University of Chicago Press.

24 For a review see Trainor, L. J., & Zatorre, R. J. (2016). The neurobiology of musical expectations. In S. Hallam, I. Cross, & M. Thaut (eds.), *The Oxford handbook of music psychology* (pp. 285–306). Oxford: Oxford University Press.

Chapter 3

1 Bronfenbrenner, U. (2009). *The ecology of human development*. Cambridge, MA: Harvard University Press.

2 Gaunt, H., & Hallam, S. (2016). Individuality in the learning of musical skills. In S. Hallam, I. Cross, & M. Thaut (eds.), *Oxford Handbook of Music Psychology* (2nd edition, pp. 463–478). Oxford: Oxford University Press.

3 Hettema, J., & Kenrick, D. T. (1992). Models of person-situation interactions. In G. V. Caprara & G. L. Van Heck (eds.), *Modern personality psychology: Critical reviews and new directions* (pp. 393–417). New York: Harvester Wheatsheaf.

4 Byrd, A. L., & Manuck, S. B. (2014). MAOA, childhood maltreatment, and antisocial behavior: Meta-analysis of a gene-environment interaction. *Biological Psychiatry, 75*(1), 9–17.

5 Altenmüller, E. O. (2003). How many music centres are in the brain? In I. Peretz & R. Zatorre (eds.), *The cognitive neuroscience of music* (pp. 346–356). Oxford: Oxford University Press.

6 Munte, T. F., Nager, W., Beiss, T. Schroeder, C., & Erne, S. N. (2003). Specialization of the specialised electrophysiological investigations in professional musicians. In G. Avanzini, C. Faienza, D. Minciacchi, L. Lopez, & M. Majno

(eds.), *The neurosciences and music* (pp. 112–117). New York: New York Academy of Sciences.

7 Parncutt, R. (2016). Prenatal development and the phylogeny and ontogeny of musical behaviour. In S. Hallam, I. Cross, & M. Thaut (eds.), *Oxford handbook of psychology of music* (2nd edition, pp. 371–386). Oxford: Oxford University Press.

8 Trehub, S. E. (2016). Infant musicality. In S. Hallam, I. Cross, & M. Thaut. *Oxford handbook of psychology of music* (2nd edition, pp. 387–398). Oxford: Oxford University Press.

9 Lamont, A. (2016). Musical development from the early years onwards. In S. Hallam, I. Cross, & M. Thaut. *Oxford handbook of psychology of music* (2nd edition, pp. 399–414). Oxford: Oxford University Press.

10 Lowther, D. (2004). An investigation of young children's timbral sensitivity. *British Journal of Music Education, 21*(1), 63–80.

11 Hargreaves, D. (1982). The development of aesthetic reactions to music. *Psychology of Music*, Special Issue, 51–54.

12 Greasley, A., & Lamont, A. (2016). Musical preferences. In S. Hallam, I. Cross, & M. Thaut. *Oxford handbook of psychology of music* (2nd edition, pp. 263–283). Oxford: Oxford University Press.

13 North, A. C., & Hargreaves, D. (2007). Lifestyle correlates of musical preference: 1. Relationships, living arrangements, beliefs, and crime. *Psychology of Music, 35*(1), 58–87.

14 Brook, O. (2013). Reframing models of arts attendance: Understanding the role of access to a venue. The case of opera in London. *Cultural Trends. 22*(2), 97–107.

15 Bennett, T., Savage, M., Silva, E. B., Warde, A., Gayo-Cal, M., & Wright, D. (2009). *Culture, class, distinction.* London: Routledge.

16 Zajonc, R. B. (1968). Attitudinal effects of mere exposure. *Journal of Personality and Social Psychology, 9*(2), 1–21.

17 Berlyne, D. E. (1971). *Aesthetics and psychobiology.* New York: Appleton-Century-Crofts.

18 Schubert, E. (2007). The influence of emotion, locus of emotion and familiarity upon preference in music. *Psychology of Music, 35,* 499–515.

19 Gembris, H. (2008). Musical activities in the third age: An empirical study with amateur musicians. In A. Daubney, E. Longhi, A. Lamont, & D. J. Hargreaves (eds.), *Musical development and learning. Conference proceedings, Second European Conference on Developmental Psychology of Music, Roehampton University, England,* 10–12 September (pp. 103–108). Hull: G.K. Publishing.

20 Creech, A., Hallam, S., McQueen, H., & Varvarigou, M. (2014). *Active ageing with music: Supporting well being in the third and fourth ages.* London: IOE Press.

21 Stebbins, R. A. (1992). *Amateurs, professionals and serious leisure.* Montreal, QC: McGill-Queen's University Press.

22 Hallam, S., & Creech, A. (eds). (2010). *Music education in the 21st century in the United Kingdom: Achievements, analysis and aspirations.* London: Institute of Education, University of London.

23 Hallam, S., & Papageorgi, I. (2016). Conceptions of musical understanding. *Research Studies in Music Education,* 38(2), 133–154.

24 Hays, T., & Minichiello, V. (2005). The contribution of music to quality of life in older people: An Australian qualitative study. *Ageing and Society,* 25(2), 261–278.

Chapter 4

1 For a review see Hallam, S., Creech, A., & Varvarigou, M. (2017). Well-being and music leisure activity through the lifespan: A psychological perspective. In R. Mantie & G. D. Smith (eds.), *Oxford handbook of music making and leisure* (pp. 31–60). Oxford: Oxford University Press.

2 For a review see Lamont, A., Greasley, A., & Sloboda, J. (2016). Choosing to hear music: Motivation, process and effect. In S. Hallam, I. Cross, & M. Thaut (eds.), *The Oxford handbook of music psychology* (2nd edition, pp. 711–724). Oxford: Oxford University press.

3 DeNora, T. (2000). *Music in everyday life.* Cambridge, MA: Cambridge University Press.

4 For a review see Hargreaves, D. J., MacDonald, R., & Miell, D. (2016). Musical identities. In S. Hallam, I. Cross, & M. Thaut (eds.), *The Oxford Handbook of Music Psychology* (2nd edition, pp. 759–774). Oxford: Oxford University press.

5 Selfhout, M. H. W., Delsing, M. J., ter Bogt, M. H., & Meeus, W. H. J. (2008). Heavy metal and hip-hop style preferences and externalizing problem behaviour: A two-wave longitudinal study. *Youth and Society,* 39, 435–452.

6 Scheel, K. R., & Westefeld, J. S. (1999). Heavy metal music and adolescent suicidality: An empirical investigation. *Adolescence,* 34, 253–273.

7 Boer, D., Fischer, R., Gürkan, H., Abubakar, A., Njenga, J., & Zenger, M. (2012). Young people's topography of musical functions: Personal, social

and cultural experiences with music across genders and six societies. *International Journal of Psychology*, 47, 355–369.

8 Hays, T., & Minichiello, V. (2005). The contribution of music to quality of life in older people: An Australian qualitative study. *Ageing and Society*, 25(2), 261–278.

9 For a review see Hallam, S., & MacDonald, R. (2016). The effects of music in community and educational settings. In S. Hallam, I. Cross, & M. Thaut (eds.), *The Oxford handbook of music psychology* (2nd edition, pp. 775–787). Oxford: Oxford University press.

10 Stebbins, R. (1992). *Amateurs, professionals, and serious leisure.* Montreal & Kingston, Canada: McGill-Queens University Press.

11 Keown, D. J. (2015). A descriptive analysis of film music enthusiasts' purchasing and consumption behaviours of soundtrack albums: An exploratory study. *Psychology of Music*, 1–15.

12 Pitts, S. E., & Burland, K. (2013). Listening to live jazz: An individual or social act? *Arts Marketing: An International Journal*, 3(1), 7–20.

13 Bennett, T., Savage, M., Silva, E. B., Warde, A., Gayo-Cal, M., & Wright, D. (2009). *Culture, Class, Distinction.* London: Routledge.

14 Audience Agency. (2013). *Audience spectrum.* www.theaudienceagency.org. Accessed on 27–08–17.

15 Lacher, K. T., & Mizerski, R. (1994). An exploratory study of the responses and relationships involved in the evaluation of, and in the intention to purchase new rock music. *Journal of Consumer Research*, 21(2), 366–380.

16 Molteni, L., & Ordanini, A. (2003). Consumption patterns, digital technology and music downloading. *Long Range Planning*, 36, 389–406.

17 Werner, D. (1984). *Amazon journey; An anthropologist's year among Brazil's Mekranoti Indians.* New York: Simon and Schuster.

18 For a review see Cohen, A. J. (2016). Music in performance arts: Film, theatre and dance. In S. Hallam, I. Cross, & M. Thaut (eds.), *The Oxford handbook of music psychology* (2nd edition, pp. 725–744). Oxford: Oxford University press.

19 For a review see North, A. C., Hargreaves, D. J., & Krause, A. E. (2016). Music and consumer behaviour. In S. Hallam, I. Cross, & M. Thaut (eds.), *The Oxford handbook of music psychology* (2nd edition, pp. 789–803). Oxford: Oxford University press.

20 Garlin, F. V., & Owen, K. (2006). Setting the tone with the tune: A meta-analytic review of the effects of background music in retail settings. *Journal of Business Research*, 59(6), 755–764.

Chapter 5

1 Jowett, B. (translater). (1888). *The republic of Plato* (p. 88). Oxford: Clarendon Press.

2 Hallam, S. (2001). *The power of music*. London: Performing Rights Society.

3 Hallam, S. (2010). The power of music: Its impact of the intellectual, personal and social development of children and young people. *International Journal of Music Education*, 38(3), 269–289.

4 For a review see Hallam, S. (2014). *The power of music: A research synthesis of the impact of actively making music on the intellectual, social and personal development of children and young people*. London: International Music Education Research Centre (iMerc), University College London, Institute of Education.

5 Huppert, F. A., & So, T. T. (2013). Flourishing across Europe: Application of a new conceptual framework for defining well-being. *Social Indicators Research*, 110(3), 837–861.

6 Steverink, N., & Siegwart, L. (2006). Which social needs are important for subjective well-being? What happens to them with aging? *Psychology and Aging*, 21, 281–290.

7 Clift, S., Hancox, G., Staricoff, R., & Whitmore, C. (2008). *Singing and health: A systematic mapping and review of non-clinical research*. Folkestone, UK: Sidney de Haan Research Centre for Arts and Health, Canterbury Christ Church University.

8 Creech, A., Hallam, S., Varvarigou, M., & McQueen, H. (2014). *Active ageing with music: Supporting wellbeing in the third and fourth ages*. London: Institute of Education Press.

9 Kreutz, G., Quiroga Murcia, C., & Bongard, S. (2012). Psychoneuroendocrine research on music and health. In R. MacDonald, G. Kreutz, & L. Mitchell (eds.), *Music, health and wellbeing* (pp. 457–490). Oxford: Oxford University Press.

10 Loewy, J. (2014). *First sounds: NICU rhythm, breath and lullaby research and practice*, Paper presented at the conference The Neueosciences and Music – V: Cognitive stimulation and rehabilitation, 29th May to June 1st, Grand Theatre/Palais des Ducs, Dijon.

11 Preti, C., & McFerran, K. (2014). Music to promote children's well-being during illness and hospitalization. In G. E. McPherson (ed.), *The child as musician*. Oxford: Oxford University Press.

12 MacDonald, R. A. R., Kreutz, G., & Mitchell, L. (eds). (2012). Music, health and wellbeing. New York: Oxford University Press.

13 Pasiali, V. (2012). Supporting child-parent interaction: Music therapy as an intervention for promoting mutually responsive orientation, Journal of Music Therapy, 48(3), 303–334.

14 Creech, A., González-Moreno, P., Lorenzino, L., & Waitman, G. (2016). El Sistema and Sistema-inspired programmes: A literature review. London: Institute of Education, for Sistema Global.

15 Dingle, G. A., Brander, C., Ballantyne, J., & Baker, F. A. (2012). To be heard: The social and mental health benefits of choir singing for disadvantaged adults. Psychology of Music, 41, 405–421.

16 Faulkner, S., Wood, L., Ivery, P., & Donovan, R. (2012). It is not just music and rhythm . . . Evaluation of a drumming-based intervention to improve the social well-being of alienated youth. Children Australia, 37(1), 31–39.

17 Qa Research. (2012). Young people not in education, employment or training (NEET) and music making. London: Youth Music.

18 Henley, J., Caulfield, L. S., Wilson, D., & Wilkinson, D. J. (2012). Good vibrations: Positive change through social music making. Music Education Research, 14(4), 499–520.

19 Hallam, S., Creech, A., & McQueen, H. (2017). Teachers' perceptions of the impact on students of the musical futures approach. Music Education Research, 19(3), 263–275.

20 Odena, O. (2010). Practitioners' views on cross-community music education projects in Northern Ireland: Alienation, socio-economic factors and educational potential. British Educational Research Journal, 36, 83–105.

21 Rabinowitch, T. C., Cross, I., & Burnard, P. (2013). Long-term musical group interaction has a positive influence on empathy. Psychology of Music, 41(4), 484–498.

22 Miksza, P. (2010). Investigating relationships between participation in high school music ensembles and extra-musical outcomes: An analysis of the education longitudinal study of 2002 using bio-ecological development model. Bulletin of the Council for Research in Music Education, 186, 7–25.

23 Geretsegger, M., Elefant, C., Mossler, K. A., & Gold, S. (2014). Randomised control trial of improvisational music therapy's effectivenss for children with autism spectrum disorders (TIME-A): A study protocol. BMC Paediatrics, 12, 2.

24 Dillon, L. (2010). *Looked after children and music making: An evidence review*. London: Youth Music.

25 Waaktaar, T., Christie, H. J., Inger Helmen Borge, A., & Torgersen, S. (2004). How can young people's resilience be enhanced? Experiences from a clinical intervention project. *Clinical Child Psychology and Psychiatry*, 9(2), 167–183.

26 Daykin, N., Moriarty, Y., Viggiani, N., & Pilkington, P. (2011). *Evidence review: Music making with young offenders and young people at risk of offending*. Bristol and London: University of West of England/Youth Music.

27 Fancourt, D., Ockelford, A., & Belai, A. (2014). The psychoneuroimmunological effects of music: A systematic review and a new model. *Brain, Behaviour and Immunology*, 36, 15–26.

28 Mainka, S., Spintge, R., & Thaut, M. (2016). Music therapy in medical and neurological, rehabilitation settings. In S. Hallam, I. Cross, & M. Thaut (eds.), *Oxford handbook of music psychology* (pp. 857–873). Oxford: Oxford University Press.

29 Wheeler, B. L. (2016). Research in music therapy. In S. Hallam, I. Cross, & M. Thaut (eds.), *Oxford handbook of music psychology* (pp. 835–855). Oxford: Oxford University Press.

30 Clift, S. (2012). Singing, wellbeing and health. In R. A. R. MacDonald, G. Kreutz, & L. Mitchell (eds.), *Music, Health and Wellbeing* (pp. 111–124). Oxford: Oxford University Press.

Chapter 6

1 McPherson, G., & Hallam, S. (2009). Musical potential. In: Hallam, S. Cross, I, & Thaut, M. (eds.), *Oxford handbook of music psychology* (pp. 225–254). Oxford: Oxford University Press.

2 Morley, I. (2013). *The prehistory of music: Evolutionary origins and archaeology of human musicality*. Oxford: Oxford University Press.

3 Shuter-Dyson, R. (1999). Musical ability. In D. Deutsch (ed.), *The psychology of music* (pp. 627–651). New York: Harcourt Brace and Company.

4 Pulli, K., Karma, K., Norio, R., Sistonen, P. Goring, H. H. H., & Jarvela, I. (2008). Genome-wide linkage scan for loci of musical aptitude in Finnish families: Evidence for a major locus at 4q22. *Journal of Medical Genetics*, 45:451–456. doi: 10.1136/jmg.2007.056366 451

5 Ukkola-Vuoti, L., Oikkonen, J., Buck, G., Blancer, C., Raijas, P., Karma, K., Lähdesmäki, H., & Järvelä, I. (2013). Genome-wide copy number variation analysis in extended families and unrelated individuals characterized for musical aptitude and creativity in music. *PLOS ONE*, 8(2), e56356.

6 Schlaug, G. (2003). The brain of musicians. In I. Peretz & R. Zatorre (eds.), *The cognitive neuroscience of music* (pp. 366–381). Oxford: Oxford University Press.

7 Loui, P. (2016). Absolute pitch. In S. Hallam, I. Cross, & M. Thaut (eds.), *Oxford handbook of music psychology* (pp. 81–94). Oxford: Oxford University Press.

8 Miyazaki, K., & Ogawa, Y. (2006). Learning absolute pitch by children: A cross sectional study. *Music Perception*, 42(1), 63–78.

9 Mottron, L., Dawson, M., & Soulieres, I. (2009). Enhanced perception in savant syndrome: Patterns, structure and creativity. *Philosophical Transactions of the Royal Society*, 364, 1385–1391. doi: 10.1098/rstb.2008.0333

10 McPherson, G. E., & Lehmann, A. (2012). Exceptional musical abilities – child prodigies. In G. E. McPherson & G. Welch (eds.), *Oxford handbook of music education* (pp. 31–50). New York: Oxford University Press.

11 Ruthsatz, J., & Detterman, D. K. (2003). An extraordinary memory: The case study of a musical prodigy. *Intelligence*, 31, 509–518.

12 Vandervert, L. A. (2009). Working memory, the cognitive functions of the cerebellum and the child prodigy. In L. V. Shavinina (ed.), *International handbook of giftedness* (pp. 295–316). New York: Springer.

13 Glaser, R., & Chi, M. T. H. (1988). Overview. In M. T. H. Chi, R. Glaser, & M. J. Farr (eds.), *The nature of expertise*. Hillsdale, NJ: Lawrence Erlbaum associates.

14 Hallam, S. (2010). Transitions and the development of expertise. *Psychology Teaching Review*, 16(2), 3–32.

15 Jorgensen, H., & Hallam, S. (2016). Practising. In S. Hallam, I. Cross, & M. Thaut (eds.), *Oxford handbook of music psychology* (2nd edition, pp. 449–462). Oxford: Oxford University Press.

16 Fitts, P. M., & Posner, M. I. (1967). *Human performance*. Belmont, California: Brooks Cole.

17 Altenmuller, E. O. (2003). How many music centres are in the brain? In I. Peretz & R. Zatorre (eds.), *The cognitive neuroscience of music* (pp. 346–356). Oxford: Oxford University Press.

18 Gardner, H. (1983). *Frames of mind: The theory of multiple intelligences*. New York: Basic Books.

19 Gordon, E. E. (2007). *Learning sequences in music: A contemporary music learning theory*. Chicago: GIA.

20 Hallam, S., & Prince, V. (2003). Conceptions of musical ability. *Research Studies in Music Education*, 20, 2–22.

21 Hallam, S. (2010). 21st century conceptions of musical ability. *Psychology of Music*, July, 38(3), 308–330.

22 Müllensiefen, D., Gingras, B., Musil, J., & Stewart, L. (2014). The musicality of non-musicians: An index for assessing musical sophistication in the general population. *PLoS ONE*, 9(2): e89642. https://doi.org/10.1371/journal.pone.0089642

23 Hallam, S., & Gaunt, H. (2012). *Preparing for success: A practical guide for young musicians*. London: Institute of Education Press.

24 Hallam, S. (2016). Musicality. In G. McPherson (ed.), *The child as musician: A handbook of musical development* (2nd edition, pp. 69–80). Oxford: Oxford University Press.

Chapter 7

1 Webb, M., & Seddon, F. A. (2012). Musical instrument learning, music ensembles, and musicianship in a global and digital age. In G. E. McPherson & G. F. Welch (eds.), *The Oxford handbook of music education, Volume 1* (pp. 752–768). Oxford: Oxford University Press.

2 Ericsson, K. A., Krampe, R. T., & Tesch-Römer, C. (1993). The role of deliberate practice in the acquisition of expert performance. *Psychological Review*, 100(3), 363–406.

3 Sudnow, D. (1978). *Ways of the hand: The organisation of improvised conduct*. London: Routledge and Kegan Paul.

4 Hallam, S. (2010). Transitions and the development of expertise. *Psychology Teaching Review*, 16(2), 3–32.

5 Jorgensen, H., & Hallam, S. (2016). Practising. In S. Hallam, I. Cross, & M Thaut (eds.), *Oxford handbook of music psychology* (2nd edition, pp. 449–462). Oxford: Oxford University Press.

6 Hallam, S., Rinta, T., Varvarigou, M., Creech, A., Papageorgi, I., & Lani, J. (2012). The development of practising strategies in young people. *Psychology of Music*, 40(5), 652–680.

7 Blacking, J. (1973). *How musical is man?* Seattle: University of Washington Press.

8 Hallam, S., Creech, A., Papageorgi, I., Gomes, T., Rinta, T., Varvarigou, M., & Lanipekun, J. (2016). Changes in motivation as expertise develops: Relationships with musical aspirations. *Musicae Scientiae*, 20(4), 528–550.

9 Creech, A. (2016). The role of the family in supporting learning. In S. Hallam, I. Cross, & M. Thaut (eds.), *Oxford handbook of music psychology* (2nd edition, pp. 493–507). Oxford: Oxford University Press.

10 Hallam, S. (2016). Motivation to learn. In S. Hallam, I. Cross, & M. Thaut (eds.), *Handbook of psychology of music* (2nd edition, pp. 479–492). Oxford: Oxford University Press.

11 Hallam, S. (2010). 21st century conceptions of musical ability. *Psychology of Music*, 38(3), 308–330.

12 Davidson, J. (2012). The role of bodily movement in learning and performing music: Application for education. In G. E. McPherson & G. F. Welch (eds.), *The Oxford handbook of music education*, Volume 1 (pp. 769–783). Oxford: Oxford University Press.

13 Papageorgi, I., & Kopiez, R. (2012). Psychological and physiological aspects of learning to perform. In G. E. McPherson & G. F. Welch (eds.), *The Oxford handbook of music education*, Volume 1 (pp. 731–751). Oxford: Oxford University Press.

14 Altenmüller, E. (2006). Hirnphysiologische Grundlagen des Übens [Neurophysiological foundations of practising]. In U. Mahlert (ed.), *Handbuch Üben* (pp. 47–66). Wiesbaden: Breitkopf & Härtel.

Chapter 8

1 Hallam, S. (2014). *The power of music: A research synthesis of the impact of actively making music on the intellectual, social and personal development of children and young people*. London: iMERC.

2 Moreno, S., & Besson, M. (2006). Musical training and language-related brain electrical activity in children. *Psychophysiology*, 43, 287–291.

3 Rauscher, F. H., & Hinton, S. C. (2011). Music instruction and its diverse extra-musical benefits. *Music Perception*, 29, 215–226.

4 Strait, D., & Kraus, N. (2011). Playing music for a smarter ear: Cognitive, perceptual, and neurobiological evidence. *Music Perception: An interdisciplinary journal*, 29(2), 133–146.

5 Putkinen, V., Tervaniemi, M., & Huotilainen, M. (2013). Informal musical activities are linked to auditory discrimination and attention in 2–3-year-old children: An event-related potential study. *European Journal of Neuroscience*, 37(4), 654–661.

6 Moreno, S., Marques, C., Santos, A., Santos, M., Castro, S. L., & Besson, M. (2009). Musical training influences linguistic abilities in 8-year-old children: More evidence for brain plasticity. *Cerebral Cortex*, 19, 712–723.

7 Hallam, S. (2017). The impact of making music on aural perception and language skills: A research synthesis. *London Review of Education*, 15(3), 388–406.

8 Moreno, S., Friesen, D., & Bialystok, E. (2011). Effect of music training on promoting preliteracy skills: Preliminary causal evidence. *Music Perception*, 29, 165–172.

9 Corrigall, K. A., & Trainor, L. J. (2011). Associations between length of music training and reading skills in children. *Music Perception*, 29, 147–155.

10 Miendlarzewska, E. A., & Trost, W. J. (2014). How musical training affects cognitive development: Rhythm, reward and other modularing variables. *Frontiers of Neuroscience*, 20(7), 279. doi: 10.3389/fnins.2013.00279

11 Cohen, M. A., Evans, K. K., Horowitz, T. S., & Wolfe, J. M. (2011). Auditory and visual memory in musicians and nonmusicians. *Psychonomic Bulletin & Review*, 18, 586–591.

12 Hetland, L. (2000). Learning to make music enhances spatial reasoning. *Journal of Aesthetic Education*, 34(3/4), Special Issue, The Arts and Academic Achievement: What the evidence shows (Autumn –Winter, 2000), 179–238.

13 Črnčec, A., Wilson, S. J., & Prior, M. (2006). The cognitive and academic benefits of music to children: Facts and fiction. *Educational Psychology: An International Journal of Experimental Educational Psychology*, 26(4), 579–594.

14 Vaughn, K. (2000). Music and mathematics: Modest support for the oft-claimed relationship. *Journal of Aesthetic Education*, 34(3–4), 149–166.

15 Jaschke, A. C., Eggermont, L. H. P., Honing, H., & Scherder, E. J. A. (2013). Music education and its effect on intellectual abilities in children: A systematic review. *Reviews in the neurosciences*, 24(6), 665–675.

16 Schellenberg, E. G. (2011). Examining the association between music lessons and intelligence. *British Journal of Psychology*, 102, 283–302.

17 Hurwitz, I., Wolff, P. H., Bortnick, B. D., & Kokas, K. (1975). Non-musical effects of the Kodaly music curriculum in primary grade children. *Journal of Learning Disabilities*, 8, 45–52.

18 Schellenberg, E. G. (2004). Music lessons enhance IQ. *Psychological Science*, 15(8), 511–514.

19 Costa-Giomi, E., & Ryan, C. (2007). *The benefits of music instruction: What remains years later.* Paper presented at the Symposium for Research in Music Behaviour, March, Baton Rouge, LO.

20 Sluming, V., Barrick, T., Howard, M., Cezayirli, E., Mayes, A., & Roberts, N. (2002). Voxel – based morphometry reveals increased gray matter density in Broca's area in male symphony orchestra musicians. *Neuroimage*, 17(3), 1613–1622.

21 Nutley, S. B., Darki, F., & Klingberg, T. (2013). Music practice is associated with development of working memory during childhood and adolescence. *Frontiers in Human Neuroscience*, 7, 926. doi.org/10.3389%2Ffnhum.2013.00926

22 Moreno, S., Bialystok, E., Barac, R., Schellenberg, E. G., Cepeda, N. J., & Chau, T. (2011). Short-term music training enhances verbal intelligence and executive function. *Psychological Science*, 22, 1425–1433.

23 Hallam, S., & Rogers, K. (2016). The impact of instrumental learning on attainment at age 16: A pilot study. *British Journal of Music Education*, 33(3), 247–261.

24 Creech, A., Gonzalez-Moreno, P., Lorenzino, L., Waitman, G. et al. (2016). *El Sistema and Sistema-inspired programmes: A literature review of research, evaluation and critical debates* (2nd edition). San Diego, California: Sistema Global.

25 Corrigall, K. A., Schellenberg, E. G., & Misura, N. M. (2013). Music training, cognition, and personality. *Frontiers in Psychology*, 4: 222. doi: 10.3389/fpsyg.2013.00222

26 Creech, A., Hallam, S., Varvarigou., & McQueen, H. (2014). *Active ageing with music: Supporting well-being in the third and fourth ages.* London: IOE Press.

Printed in the United States
by Baker & Taylor Publisher Services